Additional Praise for *Waging Peace*

"*Waging Peace* is truly touching and inspiring. Diana Oestreich's story of being on the battlefield, surrounded by all sorts of life-threatening unknowns, yet choosing to shed fear and look through purely humane glasses made all the difference in the world. I sincerely hope others will follow in her footsteps and help add more smiles and spread more peace."
—Abe Al-Qudah, former president of the Islamic Center of Twin Ports

"Diana tells a powerful story about faith and love. Her journey of self-discovery and fighting to stand up and live her beliefs is truly inspiring. This book made me smile, cry, and feel hope all at the same time. Diana's book encourages us all to evaluate our ability to live by our own moral code."
—Beth Al-Qudah, member, Islamic Center of Twin Ports

"*Waging Peace* should be required reading for all those committed to creating a world rooted in an ethic of love. It is a poignant story of deep personal transformation forged through the trauma and horror of war and shaped by the power of relationship. Oestreich invites us to journey with her as she learns and then lives the value of peace by introducing us to the people and places who served as her guides. What a heartbreakingly beautiful gift it is to walk alongside her."
—Rev. Jen Bailey, founder and executive director, Faith Matters Network

"'Love never fails.' Oestreich's *Waging Peace* invites us to believe those words as never before. The world is barricaded behind walls of shame and 'otherizing,' and only tender love can scale those walls. On the other side, we find our shared humanity, a reverence for complexity, and a longing to be practitioners of this dangerous hope that only chooses love. This book helps you scale the walls."
—Gregory J. Boyle, S.J., founder of Homeboy Industries, author of the *New York Times* bestseller, *Tattoos on the Heart: The Power of Boundless Compassion*

"A courageous, moving, true story by a brave, truthful woman, about what it means to be a Christian, a soldier, and a peacemaker. Diana Oestreich breaks down all manner of falsehoods, telling tales that are, on one page, profoundly inspiring and, on the next page, deeply distressing. We need many more such witnesses in the world today. What a gift to us all that Diana has written this book."
—Lee C. Camp, author of *Scandalous Witness: A Little Political Manifesto for Christians*, and host of the Tokens Show

"Diana is a rare gem who shows up authentically in person, online, and in her writing. If, like me, you feel far from war, this is a must-read. *Waging Peace* is about creating longer tables instead of building higher fences, and as Christ-followers, isn't that the whole point?"
—Manda Carpenter, author of *Space: An Invitation to Create Sustainable Rhythms of Work, Play, and Rest*

"Diana's story of leaning into the extravagantly dangerous reality of loving her enemies as a soldier in the Iraq War is a story for our time. With gut-wrenching honesty, Diana takes on the overly simplified, preachy admonition to 'love your enemy' that so many of us learned in Sunday school and shows us how difficult and worthwhile it is to leave our prison of self-preservation and step into the terrifying freedom of loving without limits."

—Courtney Christenson, writer, activist, peacemaker, and founder of Sparks and Matches

"Books are believed to be most impactful when they have the potential to change the heart of the person reading them. But when the words of a book have the power to change the trajectory of a whole generation, to take the wounds of violence and war and pick up weapons of peace and love, that's when we all should turn our night-lights on, stretch open the pages, and dive in with a posture to be changed and humbled. Diana Oestreich hasn't just written a book; she's given us a map. From real experiences on the front lines of the Iraq War to a redemption story that will help lead us all to a more whole world. Forever humbled."

—Toni J. Collier, peacemaker and founder of Broken Crayons Still Color

"*Waging Peace* is an invitation to take the life-changing love of God seriously. With vivid stories and honest meditations from the deserts of Iraq to wooden church pews of the Midwest, Diana brings us on her journey of dismantling tightly held notions of God and country. This book will embrace your humanity and never let you go. For those who wonder if there's a way out of hate and violence, for those who ache for permission to see the fullness of God beyond borders or bloodlines, this book is for you. In a volatile world full of hate, violence, and war, *Waging Peace* shows that another way is possible. Rooted in love and told with unflinching honesty, this book is a compass guiding us out of hate, pointing toward a God big enough for us all."

—Kayla Craig, founder and co-host of Upside Down Podcast

"In this warm, compelling, and provocative book, Diana Oestreich offers us her own deeply personal story as an invitation to live a generous life governed by love. Prepare to be drawn into her journey, and both inspired and challenged by her choices."
—Todd Deatherage, co-founder of The Telos Group

"As Christian nationalism swells across America, and as American Christians are encouraged to militarize their faith, we all deeply need the voice of Diana Oestreich, an American military veteran who has dedicated her post-war life to peacemaking. From her desperate mission to save a baby boy's life in small-town Iraq, to her commitment to raising her white and black sons to fight for justice, Oestreich inspires, encourages, and urges us all to make the sometimes-difficult choice to love first, even in war."
—Angela Denker, author of *Red State Christians*

"This book could change our country, starting with me and you. Peacemakers run toward conflict, and that's exactly what Diana does in *Waging Peace*. Rarely do we change our minds on divisive issues without personal stories and friendship. Every word expanded my humanity and heart. I'm with Diana, squarely planting my feet in love."
—April L. Diaz, founder and lead warrior, Ezer + Co.

"Diana Oestreich has written a brave book. She deploys to Iraq as a soldier, comes home to Minnesota as a peacemaker, and returns to Iraq as an activist. Through stories of everyday moments as a young medic and then a mom, Oestreich describes a journey of reconciling

deep beliefs in God, country, and family with realities of trauma, fear, and injustice. This is what it means to lead an examined life."
—Deborah Fallows, co-author of *Our Towns: A 100,000-Mile Journey into the Heart of America*

"'God wasn't calling out my bad theology; God was confronting my unlove.' This line from Diana's book evoked in me an 'ouch' and a 'hallelujah' at the same time. You'll encounter a lot of those moments throughout this prophetic but gentle call to love. I think if the church really understood what loving your neighbor looks like as Diana beautifully and heartbreakingly describes it, we might really see peace on earth. Thank you, Diana, for gifting us with a labor of love."
—Susie Gamez, speaker and minister

"Diana Oestreich is all things bold and courageous as she leads our culture into a conversation we so desperately need. If you want to learn how to see the world through a lens of love, uproot deeply embedded cultural narratives, and gain the tools to wage peace in the name of Jesus, then read this book. If we lean into this story and learn from Diana's example, I truly believe our world will never be the same."
—Hannah Gronowski, speaker, author, founder & CEO of Generation Distinct

"This book is for those who want to learn how to truly live, not just survive. Oestreich invites us into a dangerous hope. Her compelling story and unique perspective from both sides of war dare us to believe that we have something extravagant to give instead of something priceless to protect. Her poignant invitation to choose preemptive love over fear imparts to us the courage to face what's broken first in ourselves and then in the systems affecting those around us. She

knows firsthand that only love has the power to change us and our hurting world, so like a neon sign this timely book points us to the way of waging peace through extravagant love."
—Kellie Haddock, singer/songwriter

"In our polarized time, vulnerability is the most radical act of courage. It breaks down the walls between 'us' and 'them' and allows us to truly see, listen to, and love each other. In *Waging Peace*, Diana Oestreich brings us on a truly vulnerable journey. She fearlessly explores the complex tensions in her identity and her duty—to country, God, family, and self. Her writing brings us deep into her world; we can taste the sand in the air and feel the heaviness of the hot sun weighing down our uniforms. We are there with her, holding the hands of those she is sworn to protect and serve. In this book, love is palpable, it is contagious, and it inspires the reader 'to run toward love as if your life depends on it.'"
—Ashley Hanson, Founder, Department of Public Transformation; Obama Foundation Fellow

"I thought I knew war because I lived in it. I thought I knew the struggle between what I believe and what my duty and responsibility to my community are—until I read this book. For anyone who wants to know what it feels like to live out your own beliefs, the things that matter the most, the things that travel across faith and duty, across cultures and communities—I recommend this book. No borders or seas or religion or race can limit the message in it. Thank you, Diana, for being the human God wants us all to be, whatever our faith or race or language—for showing us what it means to see and love each other as humans."
—Ihsan Ibraheem, program documentarian, Preemptive Love Coalition, and Iraq War survivor

"We can choose how we fight the injustices of this world, and *Waging Peace* gives us a blueprint. After reading this book, you will be compelled to step up and step into the pain and brokenness of this world with new eyes and a new heart for loving people—your neighbor and your enemy. This is the way the world will be transformed toward peace."
—Lisa Jernigan, co-founder of Amplify Peace and co-host of GirlfriendIT podcast

"Diana Oestreich shares her story of transformation at a time when the world needs such vulnerable testimony. Lest we believe change is no longer possible, that we have gone too far down the path of war and hate, *Waging Peace* is the medicine we need to restore ourselves to the path of peacemaking."
—Whitney Kimball Coe, director of national programs, Center for Rural Strategies

"During a time in history when we're witnessing more physical and ideological walls being built, *Waging Peace* beautifully advocates for building fewer walls, longer bridges, and bigger tables. Diana masterfully blends her story with a vision for what is possible once we embrace a theology and a lifestyle of lavishing peace on friends and enemies alike. I pray we'll read this book and begin putting the truths it contains into practice immediately."
—Nick Laparra, environmentalist, speaker, investigative journalist, and founder of Let's Give a Damn

"In faith pursuits, the simplest commitments always get closer to the heart of things. That's what I found in Diana's *Waging Peace*. Summed up with clarity rising from living into truth, not just talking about it, she offers this message: 'Love first. Love always. Neighbors

and enemies. It's possible, even in life's most challenging moments.' Diana's story could not be more relevant and needed, here and now, where fear and division find constant justification to see even our neighbors as enemies. This book inspires. I feel a resonant sense of gratitude for this voice at this time."
—John Paul Lederach, professor emeritus, University of Notre Dame

"Diana Oestreich's storytelling is heartbreakingly beautiful. She brings us to the frontlines of the war in Iraq and gives an insider view of her personal journey to becoming a peacemaker. Her words are infused with pain and truth, yet balanced with hope and joy. Her stories remind us that we all have the opportunity to undergo heart transformation when we see our enemies as neighbors, the 'other' as a friend."
—Leisa McDonald, Associate Director of Global Outreach, Central Christian Church, Phoenix

"Diana is still tending to our wounds, but now she is healing our hearts. I am so grateful for Diana's courage as she offers her story, her pain, and her path so we may follow her into new territories. As we set out to wage peace together, we need the ones who know the way."
—Idelette McVicker, founder, *SheLoves* magazine

"Diana Oestreich's powerful memoir takes readers along as she and her fellow soldiers of a Minnesota Army National Guard unit take part in the invasion of Iraq in 2003. Diana holds nothing back as she tries to reconcile the brutality of war with the religious and patriotic values of her upbringing. This is a book of courage and insight that

brings us to a deeper understanding of love, 'the most powerful weapon of all.'"
—Dr. Thomas Morgan, director Alworth Center for the Study of Peace & Justice, College of St. Scholastica, Duluth, Minnesota, and veteran of the Vietnam War

"Diana Oestreich's *Waging Peace* gives readers an intimate look into the complexity of war and how finding peace within our own stories affords us the opportunity to live with boldness and risk. A practitioner of dangerous hope, Oestreich's story is nothing less than compelling and captivating. And a reminder that we all have the power to love more expansively than we ever imagined possible."
—Rev. Heather Mustain, Minister of Missions and Advocacy, Wilshire Baptist Church, Dallas

"Maybe we can only truly learn to disarm violence, within and without, from a soldier. In *Waging Peace*, Diana Oestreich instructs us through insightful and crisp narratives she lived on the battlefield of Iraq and back home in suburban Minnesota. Violence, enemies, and fear follow us wherever we go. But so does the imperative to love, to disarm our hatreds, and to wage peace—no matter where we live. This is a story about finding freedom in unexpected places and wrestling to live it out amid wartime. It is about the freedom to lay down our life and love our enemies where the risks are real, but so are the rewards. Let this story disarm your weapons of choice and show you what it might look like to wage peace wherever you live."
—Kelley Nikondeha, author of *Defiant: What the Women of Exodus Teach Us about Freedom*

"As a Vietnam-era Marine Corps veteran, I was absorbed by Diana's story of her journey from 'patriot warrior' to true patriot as a lover

and advocate. She is a master storyteller and an artist, sharing many engaging stories from her road to transformation. As one who has been on a similar journey as a peace and justice seeker, I wholeheartedly recommend Diana's *Waging Peace*. You will agonize with her struggles, cry with her pain, be inspired by her love, and celebrate her commitment to life in its fullness for all!"
—John Pegg, vice president of Veterans for Peace Duluth Chapter; Founder of Witness for Peace Midwest.

"In this invaluable book, Diana charts a course for all of us to consider what it is we truly believe in light of the radical—but plain and unavoidable—nature and character of Jesus. What would we do if put in a similar position? What are we doing now? Don't you dare pick this book up if you're not willing to ask such dangerous questions."
—John Ray, spiritual director, The Abide Collective

"Diana Oestreich's personal transformation is laid out like bread crumbs for readers to follow without having to participate in military conflict. Diana shows us that the ultimate act of peace is to love. This book is a confession, an atonement, and an act of penance. If one soldier can emerge from such trials, then there is hope for us all to conquer fear. At the same time, it is an instructional manual on how humans can be more humane regardless of circumstance."
—Garett Reppenhagen, US Army Iraq veteran, and Executive Director of Veterans for Peace

"Diana Oestreich truly understands that war is a choice, and it's a choice we don't have to make anymore. Read this book and join the community of peacemakers from every corner of the world who believe that peace is not only possible but imperative."
—Jason Russell, co-founder of Invisible Children

"This is a story of courage, bravery, and love—a powerful narrative of integrity and overcoming fear. This book is like a manual for how we all have the potential to be the story we wish to see in the world."
—Kiran Singh Sirah, president, International Storytelling Center

"Diana Oestreich's story is bigger than the radical transformation she experienced in Iraq. It's bigger than her awakening, or even your awakening, to peace. In this book, Oestreich models for each one of us what it looks like to refuse to view any 'other' as 'enemy.' If you want to walk in the way of Jesus, you can practice what you discover here, boots on the ground—at the library, in the grocery store, and at the airport. Diana's story can transform your own."
—Margot Starbuck, author of *Small Things with Great Love: Adventures in Loving Your Neighbor*

"A voyeuristic and intimate invitation into the raw, emotional tug-of-war of a daughter, a mother, a combat medic, and a friend, Diana Oestreich's open diary gives readers a peek into the dichotomy of who she was, who she became, and the struggle to align the two in a world of dualities. Diana's transformational journey showcases the ongoing challenges in the search for what it means to be 'human.'"
—Anita Sugimura Holsapple, award-winning documentary filmmaker of *Battlefield: Home— Breaking the Silence*

"In *Waging Peace*, soldier-turned-peacemaker Diana Oestreich invites us into a perilous, hopeful journey. It's the pilgrimage from unquestioned allegiance to a weapons-wielding country to the willful surrender to a cross-bearing God. As you'll soon discover, it was while peering through the crosshairs at a fabricated enemy that Oestreich learned to declare holy war on the darkest parts of her soul. The questions—and demons—that emerged for her are the very ones that hold us all captive. Reader beware: her story has the power to liberate you into the restorative revolution!"

—Jer Swigart, co-founder, The Global Immersion Project; co-author, *Mending the Divides: Creative Love in a Conflicted World*

"Diana Oestreich thought she risked all in the Iraq War, but that was nothing compared to the risk she takes with this book. By prophetically challenging our understanding of peace, she risks what few would dare: her belonging. Belonging to family, to community, to country, and to you. With these stories, she stretches out her neck and hands you the axe. Will you listen? Will you choose courage, as she does over and over? I hope so, because when someone risks everything for peace, there is only one response: drop the axe, hug the neck, and wage peace. Together."

—Matthew Willingham, humanitarian, writer, and photographer

Waging Peace

Waging Peace

One Soldier's Story of Putting Love First

Diana Oestreich

Broadleaf Books

Minneapolis

WAGING PEACE

One Soldier's Story of Putting Love First

Published in association with Books & Such Literary Management, 52 Mission
Circle (Suite 122), PMB 170, Santa Rosa, CA 95409-5370.

Some names and identifying features of people and places have been changed to
protect privacy. Timelines have been compressed, and some dialogue has been
recreated from memory.

Cover Photography: Frizi/iStock
Inset Photography: Courtesy of Diana Oestreich
Cover Design: James Kegley

Print ISBN: 978-1-5064-6370-4
Ebook ISBN: 978-1-5064-6371-1

For all who are breaking silence
and telling their stories.
May you use your voice, because the world needs it.

I'm with you.

Contents

Author's Note

I lived these stories seventeen years ago. I cannot tell you they are fact—only that they are the truth as I know it. This book is a patchwork quilt of my experiences, the memories I carry, and the biased lens that I came into the world with. If I waited another twenty years to write these stories, I would likely tell them in a different way, because I am (and we all are) always changing.

"Life can only be understood backwards, but it must be lived forwards," said Søren Kirkegaard. When I look at my twenty-three-year-old self, who thought she had the market cornered on rightness and goodness, it's hard not to cringe. Here's to cringing and to honesty, so we can let ourselves grow forward and grow into love. Let's share with others the goodness that we hold so tightly in our own hands.

Maybe by telling you my story, I can enable you to see yours better. Maybe then, when you look at the person you've grown up being told to see as an enemy—of your political party, your religion, or your way of life—you'll be able to see a little of yourself in that person.

In the comic books my children love, the superheroes have origin stories that tell us how they became who they are today. This book is my origin story; it tells of the places where I began. But it's not where I will end.

I hope it's not where you end, either.

Foreword

Over the last few years, after reading headline after headline about the violence and pain around the world, I started to feel overcome by fear and hopelessness. I want to be a person of hope—the kind of hope that has arms and legs and flesh and blood. But my fears started to tell me a story of how to respond to all that pain. I found myself squeezed into a worldly idea of how we could restrain the violence we see from ISIS and other groups that are causing so much pain and havoc. I had been squeezed into believing the best scenario would be for the bombs to fall on the right people.

Now think about that for a second: That's a hopeless prayer. That's a despairing prayer. At best, that's a worldly prayer. That's the solution the world has to offer.

Violence is a despairing cultural value. But we are people of hope.

Now is the time when we need to pray transformational prayers. We need hope. We need to hear stories that lead us into wide open spaces of transformational love. This book is one of those stories that shine a light on hope.

Diana walked into war a soldier and walked out a peacemaker. God disarmed her and asked her to pick up the most powerful weapon on the planet: self-sacrificing love. Answering God's call to love those she'd been told to see as enemies freed her to be a citizen of the Kingdom of God first and a citizen of her country second.

Loving our enemies is a revolutionary answer to the deep despair in our world. It's not just some kind of idealistic optimism. It's an invitation to become, not just to believe in, the most beautiful world possible. We become messengers of hope in a despairing world when we choose to confront violence armed with a relentless love instead of hate.

Diana is showing us the way by living out the answers to these questions:

"What if you didn't have to choose between your country and the call to love? What if there was room at the table to be both a peacemaker and a patriot? How would we be different if we laid down our lives for our enemies as fiercely as we did for our friends?"

I believe the time is now to become the antidote to the despair around us. Diana is a trustworthy guide to lead us into transforming the world around us with love. Dare to walk straight into war alongside her, because you won't be the same person afterward.

Danielle Strickland, co-founder of Infinitum, Amplify Peace, Brave Global, and Women Speakers Collective and author of *Better Together*

Acknowledgments

Jake, no one has battled harder for me. You saw all of me before I knew I was possible, before I knew this *life* was possible. Thank you for being the battle buddy who loved me into being.

Bridger and Zelalem, you make me brave. Like your beloved superheroes' origin stories, this book is your family's origin story. I wanted you to know how we came to be peacemakers. It's not over. This is only the beginning. This world is yours, to love and to fight for. I can't wait to see the magic you make of it!

Al and Lyndsey, you swooped in and showed me that unconditional love is real. Thank you forever for hink-pinks, cliff jumping, coffee marathons, and showing us how to squeeze life for all it's worth, Johnson-style.

Patti Jo, you are pure magic. Thank you for choosing to love me as a daughter. I've never seen anyone love with such abandon, joy, security, and stubborn belief in the good. You've shown me how I want to mother and grandmother.

John Ray, your pain has become bright-green resurrection stories dotting the landscape where you walk. Thank you for seeing a resurrection story in me—and for sharing Olivia.

Erin, thank you for creating beauty and justice wherever you walk. Thank you for sharing your life with me. My family had an Erin-Wilson-size hole that is now filled.

Ihsan, thank you for your stunning love, open laugh, and brave friendship. You are what the world needs more of.

Om Hassan, thank you for choosing to love me first.

Dr. Sabah Alwan, thank you for opening your door and for your friendship with me. You teach me how to delight in people and see the world from the beginning instead of the end.

Ben, thank you for leveraging your power and expertise to give me a chance to be heard. I am so grateful and proud to know someone like you.

Courtney, thank you for believing in the power of women to change the world. This book is here because you put your beliefs into action. You taught me it's OK to cry but never, ever to give up.

Matt, your belief in people and peace and beauty in the middle of darkness is a double rainbow. Thank you for walking this road together with me—and for voxing while you walk to work.

Jeremy, I am forever grateful for your phone call on that Wednesday afternoon.

Grandma Diane, I am grateful for your grit, love, and determination to walk through whatever life throws you with your chin up. Thank you for loving me and for teaching me so many things about life, like never to "throw the baby out with the bathwater."

Grandma Volley, I am grateful for your life of faith, infectious love, and squeaky hugs. Our family wouldn't be us without you.

Kelley Nikondeha and Belinda Baumen, you are authors who live lives of fierce generosity instead of scarcity. Thank you for inviting me into it and cheering me along.

Rachelle Gardner, thank you for taking a chance on me. Lisa Kloskin, thank you for seeing value in my story and making it better.

Melissa, Lauri, Natalie, Amy: thank you for being my Sisterhood of Perpetual Hope.

Kristin, Lindsey, Jess, Kayla: no boulder is moved alone. Thank you for being the women who pushed so hard to help me move mine.

Onigamiising, thank you for teaching me about the land, water, and people. This community waters my roots.

Loaves and Fishes, thank you for believing in an abundant world, where there is enough for all. Your open table reminds me that it's true.

Finally, thanks to all the undercover peacemakers who quietly shout hope and love into the place you stand. I see you, Pat from QuickTrip on Twenty-Seventh Avenue and Gary at Fourth Street Auto. You shine.

Prologue

"If you slow down or stop the convoy to avoid running over a child, you will be responsible for your fellow soldiers getting attacked. I hope you understand your duty." The commander's words stung me. I was receiving the mandatory safety briefing for the next day's 4 a.m. convoy into an active war zone in Iraq. The combination of the heat of the tent and the lateness of the hour had been pushing my eyelids closed, but now he had my full attention. Safety briefings followed the same script. We trained as we fought, so even in war, it was routine—never a surprise, until now. His words made the sleepy room of soldiers buzz as if someone had poked a beehive with a stick.

The commander went on to describe a tactic the enemy used to interrupt the American invasion of Iraq. They would push Iraqi children in front of military convoys; when the trucks slowed or stopped to avoid hitting the children, the enemy would attack the last trucks in the convoy. Being at the end of the convoy made the soldiers sitting ducks: they couldn't move forward to get away, and with no other trucks behind them, they were easily ambushed. The commander barked over the voices of a hundred soldiers in the tent, "I repeat: if you slow the convoy to avoid harming a child, you will be responsible for your battle buddies getting ambushed. If anybody isn't able to do their duty and protect their battle buddies, stand up now and identify yourself."

His words hung in the air, suspended by a growing feeling of dread. I wasn't sure I could run over a child to obey this direct order from my commander. I believed in sacrificing to serve my country, even taking a life to save a life, but this? This pricked at my conscience. I knew it wasn't an option to stand up and say—as the lone female soldier in the company—that I wouldn't put the lives of my battle buddies first and do my duty. It would be a betrayal. But getting up the next day and choosing to run over a child didn't feel possible either. Looking down at my sand-encrusted combat boots, I felt my heart pounding as I gripped the knobby seam of my dusty uniform pants. The tent was filled with a suffocating silence. No one moved.

Before I could decide whether to stand up and identify myself or stay silent and do my duty, the first sergeant's voice boomed over my head like a firing cannon: "Dismissed." A wave of soldiers shuffled to their feet and poured out of the hot, dusty tent into the night air. The moment of decision was gone, and I exhaled a small breath of cowardly relief. But I still didn't know what I would do if a child were pushed in front of my convoy the next day. I had eight hours to decide.

1

Boots on the Ground

When you experience mercy, you learn things that are hard to learn otherwise. You see things you can't otherwise see; you hear things you can't otherwise hear. You begin to recognize the humanity that resides in each of us.
—Bryan Stevenson, *Just Mercy*

Burning air assaulted my lungs as I tumbled out of the C-130 transport plane into the ink-black desert night. The engines roared like pounding waterfalls, filling up my ears while the runway lights blinked and flashed around me. I sucked in a deep breath, pulling the syrupy thick air into my lungs, while the soles of my dust-colored combat boots turned sticky on the black baked tarmac. The acrid tar smell of the heated runway singed my nose, draping itself like garland across the shoulders of the soldiers of Bravo Company. My company. One hundred soldiers huddled together, waiting to face our first thirty seconds of war. We'd boarded the transport plane in the States—what felt like days or just minutes ago—and were now poured out into a war zone. Unable to see the landscape through the darkness, we stayed frozen in place. Sand-colored uniforms clumped together like human sand castles piled on the runway, waiting for the next order. The dimming roar of the plane's engine echoed through the night air as it barreled down the runway away from us, turned the corner, and left us standing alone.

"Medic!" the first sergeant yelled over top of the whine of the departing plane. "I want every soldier to have an antidote injector kit in their hands in the next five minutes. Saddam might attack us with poisonous gas."

"Keep your gas mask at the ready," barked the sergeant as he piled a mountain of green, wax-coated boxes of chemical-antidote kits into my hands. The gas mask dangling at my hip would allow me to breathe during a chemical attack, filtering out the poison in the air, much as a charcoal filter cleans water. The antidote injectors act like a shot of adrenaline, helping the body fight off the poison's internal attack. But neither one would save you indefinitely.

The sergeant's words scraped at the raw truth: chemical warfare is a living horror show, and few survive it. The gas masks and antidote injectors equipped us with false bravado and borrowed time. When the air around you turns into a weapon, you can't outrun it. When your lungs turn into soggy pools of liquid, you can't breathe. The thought of drowning inside my own body without escape made my twenty-three-year-old knees quiver. Pushing against the ticking clock and the fear of being attacked with poisonous gas, I ripped open the tops of the boxes holding the antidote kits, cardboard tearing the skin between my knuckles. My heart beat so loud in my ears that I couldn't hear anything else around me. In the darkness, I approached each huddled group of soldiers, and into the hands of every soldier, I shoved the required antidote kit to store with their gas mask. I had just five minutes to serve one hundred soldiers needing medicine to keep them alive if the air around them turned into poison.

"Breathe in, breathe out," I told myself. And just like that, I completed my first medic task to keep my soldiers alive in wartime. The invasion of Iraq had begun for my company.

For a month before this moment, I had been training at Fort McCoy to be deployed in support of the Global War on Terror. I was taught to lie on my belly and use a twelve-inch wooden stick to find hidden improvised explosive devices and disarm them before they harmed anyone—a skill every soldier learned before we deployed to the Iraq War. Nicknamed IEDs, these devices were different from the more sophisticated version called bombs.

"Medic" was a nickname given to me, but I was a combat medic, trained to be on the field to save a life—trained to stop the bleeding and keep a soldier breathing and alive while I called in a helicopter or an ambulance to get them to a hospital. The medic backpack I carried held bandages and morphine to dull the pain, not the miracles and the reassurance my soldiers hoped for. If I could keep someone alive for the first ten minutes following a battlefield injury, they cleared the first hurdle of survival. My knees shook under the weight of putting all my training into practice. I needed to keep my soldiers alive because their families and their kids expected them to return home. Their wives and families filled up my vision, as they had filled up the gym to send us off the previous week, until I couldn't see anything else. I couldn't feel anything else.

Cold dread marched up my spine, because I was standing in a killing zone. That's what war is—a battle to see who can kill more of the other until someone folds or surrenders. Turning to take one last look at the plane as I stepped off, I understood for the first time in a real, visceral way that I might never make it back home.

* * *

Home was where I had picked up the phone two months earlier to the words that brought me here. After graduating college, I had started my first nursing job on the hospice/oncology floor at Saint Luke's Hospital. I lived with two roommates on the shore of Lake Superior and was pretty sure I'd met the man I wanted to marry. He hadn't called me since our first date, but I was an eternal optimist and had a feeling I couldn't shake about him. But on Valentine's Day, the day of the call, as I held the white plastic phone receiver up to the curve of my cheek, I heard the sergeant's voice crack like a whip: "Pack your bags and report for duty in thirty days. You are being deployed in support of the Global War on Terror." As I stood and listened, with the phone cord dangling loosely from all the times it had been stretched into three different bedrooms, I understood that I was going to war. The sergeant told me to write my will, move out of my apartment, and put my stuff in storage, because he didn't know how long I would be gone or when I would return home.

The sergeant didn't need to tell me where I was going. On TV, I had seen the bombs dropping in Iraq. The call meant the military wheels were already set in motion. The military works in reverse order. The commander in chief creates the mission and then calls up the soldiers and equipment needed to execute the mission. Calling up my unit to be deployed meant the commanding officers already knew exactly where we would be going and what mission my engineer battalion was needed for. Reporting for duty in thirty days was step one in a plan that had already been set.

This is what we had trained for, but I never believed my Army National Guard unit would get called up for active duty overseas. We deployed to flood zones or to assist in recovery after a natural disaster, not to a war. Although I was a combat medic, I couldn't imagine putting into practice all the lifesaving techniques I had learned to keep someone alive on the battlefield. I prayed I'd never have to use them.

I had been in the National Guard almost six years, since I signed up at 17 years old. My head understood what was happening. But my body wasn't catching up. I couldn't hold the weight of his words. They were like water dripping through my cupped hands; their meaning was slipping through my grasp. It didn't feel possible to leave my life in Duluth, Minnesota, with my roommates, my church, and my family. The phone felt like it had turned into lead—two hundred pounds of too much, too heavy to hold up.

When I had watched the Twin Towers fall on 9/11, sitting in nursing school, I knew the world was changing around me. Still, I didn't realize that two years later, my life would be changed by the terror of that day. My life now held a fault line—a before and an after—and I was standing at the edge. One phone call had cut me off from the life I knew and propelled me forward into a future I didn't want.

* * *

After deplaning and getting our antidote kits, we waited on the tarmac in the desert night for the bus that would take us to a cluster of tents in the desert, where we were to sleep for the night. Eventually, it arrived, we boarded, and I slid into my seat as a small sigh of relief escaped underneath my breath. My first medic task was done. As the bus pulled away from the tarmac, the bus driver turned around and mumbled through the humid midnight air, "Don't peek through the closed curtains. You'll give the snipers an easy shot."

2

Eight Hours

Sometimes the truth arrives on you and you can't get it off. That's when you realize that sometimes it isn't even an answer—it's a question. Even now, I wonder how much of my life is convinced.
—Markus Zusak, *The Book Thief*

Eight hours wasn't long enough to decide if I could follow my orders to run over a child if necessary. The convoy briefing was over, but my night was just beginning. Walking back to my tent, I kept my head down, avoiding the other soldiers joking around me. The tension crackled as everyone geared up for driving into enemy territory the next day. The more dangerous the mission, the louder the jokes—that's how we handled fear.

Rucksacks needed to be packed, gear double-checked, trucks fueled up before we rolled out at four o'clock the next morning. Inside the tent, I found my green cot, and underneath it, I lined up my medic bag, rucksack, flak vest, and nine-millimeter Beretta—ready for tomorrow's mission. I lay down on top of my sleeping bag, trying to trick myself into sleeping. The commander's words were lodged in my brain: "You have to do your duty, even if it means running over a child."

Everything I believed about being a soldier and a Christian reassured me this was okay. Soldiers did hard things. I knew that. That's why my Baptist church honored them and clapped for them. My mother and father stood up in the sanctuary on Veterans Day to be honored for their military service. And their father and brothers and cousins could stand up next to them, representing our family's commitment to enlisting. I was a third-generation Army veteran. My grandmother had sent three of her five children into basic training, and I was just one of her three grandchildren now on active duty. My family tree was like a human flagpole for the American flag.

But something was crushing my chest in a vise grip and it wouldn't let me sleep—or even breathe. As I stared up into the darkness of the green camouflage tent, my cot felt as stiff and confining as a coffin. Arms folded across my chest, I lay motionless like a corpse. I struggled to shield myself from the indecision beating me up on the inside. How could I choose between the lives of my fellow soldiers and an Iraqi child? The impossibility of the choice was breaking me apart on the inside. Whose life would I protect, and whose would I take?

Hoping no one would hear me, I whispered a tiny prayer, "Oh, God, oh, God, help me," into the dark. As I prayed for the tension in my chest to release, I heard something in the dark: "But I love them. I love them, too, Diana." I froze. The words halted the wrestling match inside me. Even though I know no words were actually spoken aloud, they seemed to echo all around me.

This was not the first time I had felt sure I was sensing God—a divine presence that was so much bigger than me. The first time I experienced it, I was ten years old at Trout Lake Bible Camp, where all the Minnesota Baptist churches sent their pale Scandinavian kids in the summer to swim, get sunburned, and accept salvation. I was clapping along in chapel, when I felt like someone turned on a light switch in the room around me, and a phrase exploded in my mind like fireworks lighting up the Fourth of July summer sky: "God's love changes everything." My ears didn't hear the words, exactly, but I felt warmth spread across my chest as I watched Divine Love change everything—repainting my thoughts and head and heart with vibrant colors. Love turned my black-and-white world into Technicolor. Everything was different, as if noticing God everywhere ignited something that hadn't been there before. The words kept dancing around me: "Everything is different because of my love."

We each experience the Divine in different ways, and I can't begin to explain the "voice" I heard that day at camp. But during my night in the Iraqi desert, I heard the same voice. And it turned my world upside down, just as it had done when I was ten years old, clapping along in the chapel. The words cut through me, challenging everything I thought I knew. "But I love them, Diana. I love them, too."

God was stepping into the middle of the darkened tent with me, but instead of comforting me, God was challenging me. But if God loved "them," what did that mean for me and my orders? Was God challenging my loyalty to the "us" that I knew and loved? My uniform, my country, and my faith community had taught me that to serve my country is to serve God. I tried to understand. If God loved an Iraqi child the same sacrificial way God loved me, what was I supposed to do in eight short hours if a child was pushed in front of the convoy? This was the first time I felt caught between what God was asking of me and what my country required of me. Wishing I was anywhere other than that tent in the middle of the desert, I squeezed my eyes tightly shut.

I thought of the place where I grew up—a town of eight thousand people deep in the pine-dotted woods of northern Minnesota, famous only for walleye fishing, giant mosquitoes, and being the hometown of Judy Garland. I wished I could return to my "no place like home," just as she had. But instead, in Iraq, the yellow sunrise was coming, bringing an impossible choice. Tears slid down my face. The threads that stitched my beliefs together were fraying at the edges. I believed God is the greatest force of love the world has ever encountered—a self-sacrificing love that remakes and restores all that's broken and loves us back to life again. I knew God commands us to love our enemies—but now, in the middle of a war?

* * *

I first learned about the sanctity of life not in the sanctuary of the church, but in a crowded meeting hall basement. My mom's friend brought a few of us fifth-graders from church to a daylong rally. We were handed red shirts with "Pro-Life" printed across the front and garbage bags for the roadside trash cleanup we would be doing after lunch. I'd never seen adults behave this way—wearing matching shirts, crowding together on metal folding chairs, drawing handmade signs, and listening to people shouting from a stage. "God made life! Only God should decide when life begins and ends!" the man at the microphone shouted, as the room erupted in a level of noise that shocked me. Around me, I saw adults cheering and clapping, heads nodding up and down with uncharacteristic enthusiasm.

After the program, we headed out to pick up trash along the highway while a gray rain misted us like potted plants. My jacket was shiny and slippery, while the wet seeped slowly into my Esprit de Corp sweatshirt underneath. We took a group photo under an Adopt a Highway sign on the side of the road with "Minnesota Pro-Life" stretched across the bottom in white block letters. I guess we cared most about protecting unborn life and the cleanliness of our city's roads.

It was my first and last pro-life rally. But the words of the man at the microphone stuck with me as I grew up. Life did seem sacred. At least to my ten-year-old self, it seemed pretty simple. If I didn't make a life, I didn't have the authority to decide when it ended. If a life wasn't mine, then it wasn't mine to take.

* * *

Sweating in the dark on my Army-issued cot, I wrestled with God's words to me. My fingers traced the black plastic letters on my shirt spelling out "Army" across my chest. I knew my loyalty was to the name on my shirt, but the idea that life is sacred echoed in my ears as loud as it had that day from the stage, and I couldn't drown it out. The kingdom of heaven I was taught to pray for and build up didn't have violence, death, or killing. How could I pray a prayer asking for "Thy kingdom come, thy will be done" while readying myself to take a life? How could I be a citizen of heaven first while being a loyal citizen of my country? Which kingdom was I going to build up? All night, I tried to reason with God: "I have to. I have to take a life to save a life." Nevertheless, God's steady voice kept saying, "But I love them, Diana, I love them, too."

That's when I realized: God loves my enemies as much as God loves me. God holds their future just as carefully as mine. And God was pleading with me, to love my enemy the way God loves them. God was asking me to give my life away, instead of taking a life. This choice would cost me. To say yes would require me to act in a way that would seem like betrayal to the people I loved the most: my

13

country, my church, and even my family. It would cost me my sense of belonging in the only places that felt like home.

My kneejerk response was "No! What will people think? I can't!" I told God it would cost me too much. I wrestled with being rejected by the people and army and country that I held in such high esteem—much higher esteem than the lives of my so-called enemies, who were also created and beloved by God. My self-preservation called out, "But what about me, God? What about my life? What about my security, my safety, my being accepted and esteemed?"

Quietly and patiently, God asked me for my allegiance, for my right to violence—the very key that granted me entrance into those places and people I loved so much. If I said yes, I would be leaving behind all the places I called home. I would be all alone—even more than I already was as a female in a company of one hundred male soldiers—in a wilderness I knew nothing about, let alone how to survive in it. Instinctively, we group together to stay alive, but I was contemplating stepping away from the only group I'd ever known.

What do you do when God steps in front of your own religious beliefs and your loyalty to your country? I had a choice to make, and I couldn't ignore it.

The next morning, as light licked the edges of the desert blackness, slowly invading the morning darkness, I stood next to my assigned truck in the convoy. The top of the truck wheel was almost at my eye level. As I shifted my medic bag across my shoulders and over my flak vest, I noticed that the chin strap on my Kevlar helmet was already soaked with the sweat dripping down my round Irish chin. My bulletproof flak vest was dotted with the medic tools I needed at the ready: trauma shears, tourniquet, pressure dressing (attached upside down so I could unsnap it with one downward swipe of my hand), two plastic tubes to prop an airway open, and a magazine pouch with extra rounds for the Beretta attached to my hip.

I could feel the weight of each tool hanging off my chest, because the dinner-plate-sized bulletproof plates that were supposed to be inserted into the flak vest were missing—a casualty of trying to mobilize so many troops at one time to launch a preemptive strike in Iraq. A preemptive strike involves attacking your enemy before they have a chance to attack you, and deploying a hundred thousand troops, including some National Guard troops like myself, at one time can cause some hiccups in the supply chain—like a shortage of bulletproof plates, bottled water, or desert combat boots.

The engines of the two-and-a-half-ton trucks spit diesel fumes into the still morning air as they roared to life next to us. Waiting for the commander to start the mandatory safety briefing before we loaded up, after wrestling with God the whole night, I surrendered. I wasn't going to run over a child, no matter what. The previous night, God had stood in front of what I had believed to be right about being a Christian and a soldier and yelled, "Stop!" God blocked my path and wouldn't let me pass, no matter how hard I tried to convince God that taking a life to save a life was what "we"—God and I—believed was right. I had given my yes to God when I was too young to know that it would challenge all my other loyalties. And I couldn't let myself get beyond the one thing I knew for sure: I wouldn't run over a child, no matter what, because God loves my enemies as much as God loves me.

I wrapped my fingers around that one truth, hoping I had the strength to hold on to it. This is who God is, and I couldn't accept the love God has for me while rejecting the love God has for my enemies. I didn't know if a child would get pushed in front of our convoy. I didn't know if a battle buddy in the last trucks in the convoy would

15

be ambushed. I didn't know how the war would change me. All I knew was that I would say yes to love.

The first sergeant's roll call broke through the noise of the 4 a.m. blackness. Desert darkness is complete; like standing in a cave underground, the blackness makes you feel blind. The responses of "Here, First Sergeant" echoed like a somber game of Marco Polo from behind and in front of me throughout the darkness. Even through the blanket of morning darkness and over the hum of the engines, I recognized each voice, even though I couldn't see anyone. We'd been together once a month for the past four years calling roll call just like this. But now, instead of standing on a polished cement floor in an armory in Wisconsin, we were standing on desert sand in Iraq, half a world away from home. Today the people who belonged to those voices were my responsibility to keep alive.

Driving north into the southern region of Iraq, we'd be on the main supply route, code-named Tampa to confuse the enemy listening in on our radio channels. Supplies keep an army fighting, and this road was the artery for half the war zone's food, water, and fuel needs. This road connected the staging area in Kuwait, and it was a soldier's first stop on their way to Baghdad.

The first sergeant began the safety briefing: "Three soldiers from Eighty-Second Airborne died yesterday from an IED explosion on MSR Tampa. Four soldiers ambushed while pulling security in the Sunni Triangle. They have not been recovered yet." Each safety briefing included an intelligence report of deaths or attacks from the day before. This was partially to keep us alert and prepare us for our mission. In addition, starting each day by hearing who died and how was a way of honoring our fallen comrades by saying their names.

Next, the first sergeant assigned each truck in the convoy a driver and assistant driver. I heard "Medic" and looked up to hear my

16

assignment: "Assistant driver to truck number five!" My knees buckled together, and tears rolled down my cheeks in the dark, washing away the tension I didn't realize I had been holding so close to the surface. Relief flooded through me. I wasn't going to be a driver today, which meant I wouldn't have to decide who lived and who died in the convoy.

Pulling open the metal door attached to the fifth truck in line, the metal already warmed by the desert air, I hoisted my medic bag above my head, pushing it up until it collapsed into the foot well of the truck. Grabbing the curved handhold with my left hand, I climbed up into the truck the way an elementary schooler struggles up the rope jungle gym. Securing my medic bag between my seat and the cooler-sized radio squatting in the middle of the truck, I punched the new channel frequency into the radio we'd use to communicate during the convoy and did a communication check while the driver did the final maintenance checklist. Busying myself with the assistant-driver jobs, I pushed my shoulders back, trying to brace myself for what was coming.

Radio check done, I leaned back into my seat, waiting for the shadowy outline of the truck in front of ours to initiate the convoy by moving forward. To stay alive in a convoy, we had one rule to follow: stay within bumper distance of the truck in front, and don't lose sight of the truck behind you. The butterflies in my stomach eased up as the convoy lurched forward. It was starting. We were moving now and wouldn't stop moving unless attacked. But what was I going to do now as a soldier in middle of a war, told by God to love my enemies?

3

Red, White, and Blue

We look at the world once, in childhood. The rest is memory.
—Louise Gluck, "Nostros"

I was in kindergarten the first time I was told to put my hand on my heart and give my allegiance away. I did it before I learned to write my name or read the word *girls* on the outside of a bathroom door—basic elementary-school survival skills. Each day began when our teacher entered the room and walked to the front of the classroom to stand next to the American flag on display. We were required to put our crayons down, push in the chairs that squeaked across the polished wooden floor, and stand beside our tables. Lifting sweaty palms to our chests, we stood proud and ready for the Pledge of Allegiance.

At the end of each school day, a yellow bus waddled down the bumpy dirt road to drop me off in front of a brown two-story house with a flag standing tall in the middle of the yard and a driveway circling around it. Even though we lived ten miles northeast of the nearest town and our house was hidden from sight down a winding dirt driveway, flying the flag mattered to my dad. He and my mother had served in the Army as air traffic controllers. They met and fell in love while stationed at a small airbase at the highest peak of the Rhön Mountains in Germany. So when I looked at the flag, I knew I was looking at something important—the root of our family history and a source of family pride.

The American flag wasn't just a part of my home and school life. It also met me on Sundays inside my country church's carved mahogany doors. When my family and I would enter the small Baptist church, I could see the organ and a black sign hanging above it with removable white letters reporting the modest attendance and offering numbers from the previous week. As we settled into our usual spot (the third pew on the left side), sunlight through the stained-glass windows streamed a rainbow into the space. And as our pastor stepped up into the yellow pine pulpit, he was flanked by two flags: the American flag and a flag I didn't recognize.

The unfamiliar flag was ivory with a red cross anchored in the center of a blue square set in the top left corner. This flag wasn't a leftover decoration from a holiday. It wasn't a Baptist or Minnesotan or Scandinavian flag, reflecting our congregation's pride. I'd recognize the Finnish and Swedish flags in a heartbeat, and the Minnesota flag looks like it should be a postage stamp. I'd seen them painted on mailboxes or plastered across bumpers of cars in the church parking lot. Only much later would I find out that the unfamiliar flag was the Christian flag. Established in 1897, this flag has its own pledge. The words are sparse and powerful: "I pledge allegiance to my flag and the Savior for whose kingdom it stands; one brotherhood uniting all mankind in service and love." The flag was designed to represent Christians all around the world uniting at a time when countries were dividing into allies and enemies.

This flag represents leaving old allegiances for a new one—a new country without borders, anticipating the way it will be in heaven. It expresses a new loyalty that includes every tribe, tongue, and nation. This kingdom citizenship doesn't stop at national borders and refuses to bow to any country created by written declarations, wars, or political power. Unlike the red, white, and blue flag that adorns schools, courthouses, and the front yard of my childhood, the Christian flag signifies a citizenship in an unseen country made by God, not humans—a country that promises an eternal home and adoption into a family united by belief instead of biology or geography.

As a child, I wondered why the Christian flag shared the church altar with the American flag. The American flag already held its place of honor outside our house of worship, in front of the courthouse, and on houses. It decorated parades, was sewn on Army uniforms and T-shirts, illustrated bumper stickers, and appeared on almost every street corner on the Fourth of July. I didn't understand much about the Christian flag because we didn't pledge our allegiance to it, stand for it, or sing any songs about it. This flag wasn't invited to our parades or displayed on our houses. My family never displayed it on the flagpole in front of our house, and it wasn't what we cheered for or waved at parades or ball games. Even a five-year-old could interpret the signs that the one we were proud of was Old Glory.

So it was that I knew how to serve my country before I knew how to serve God. I knew who we cheered, in church, and in the parades. I knew we cheered when the flag came out in school and at ball games. I saw grown-ups shuffle to stand up, no matter how old, the same way I did in my kindergarten class for the daily Pledge of Allegiance.

Despite our long history of service, my family didn't celebrate patriotic holidays with fanfare. We didn't talk about the flag often or pledge allegiance to it in my home. I wish my parents had talked more about their military service, what it meant to them, or what they thought serving God meant. No one took me aside and whispered in my ear, "I hope you go serve your country when you grow up."

The shiny mahogany pew, third row from the front under the stained-glass window, is where I learned it. My country Baptist church, with my fellow citizens of heaven, was the place where I learned to put my country first. These people inspired me with their faithfulness, fantastic Bible stories on the flannel board in Sunday school, and their deep love for me. The people I worshipped alongside in the wooden pew helped to define my understanding of whom I served when I served my country.

My church taught me the Ten Commandments, but they didn't teach me what "do not kill" means in the middle of a war zone. They didn't teach me why we seemed to think we were exempt from Jesus's command to love our enemies. That was a question I would have to wrestle with by myself, at twenty-three years old in the middle of the desert war.

4

Awaijah

*And the more they asked, the more they wondered. And the more they
wondered, the more they hoped. And the more they hoped, the more the clouds
of sorrow lifted, drifted, and burned away in the heat of a brightening sky.*
—Kelly Barnhill, *The Girl Who Drank the Moon*

We had been waging war for a couple of months when I found
myself in a dusty local village where my company of combat
engineers was rebuilding a culvert that had collapsed. After a few days
of waiting for someone to get hurt so that I could spring into action
and use my medic skills, I wandered away from the construction
site to explore the village. The main road meandered as if it had
been carved by a determined flock of sheep on a lazy afternoon stroll
weaving back and forth across the hard-packed dirt. It led to the base
of a small hill, where it widened and climbed to reveal a few scattered
dwellings. Shuttered tin, rusted to the color of bright-orange autumn
leaves, hugged knee-high walls of brown mud-encrusted brick. The
heat made my five-foot frame move in a slow-motion shuffle. Sweat

dripping down my collar weighed down my salt-whitened uniform like a ten-pound wet blanket wrapped around my shoulders.

As I shuffled down the path, I saw a corrugated door move slightly. With a metallic squeak, it opened a couple of inches. No one came out, but the door stayed open while dark pupils surrounded by intent white eyes locked on me. The woman whose eyes I could see was covered from head to toe in black; she was wearing the chador—the customary modesty cloak—over her whole body. She looked small in the doorway, but the crinkling skin around her smiling eyes revealed her age and the twinkle of someone wanting my attention. Iraqi women in this area didn't leave their homes without a male family escort. Caught in the midafternoon lull when almost everything breathing hid from the punishing sun and napped, the street was deserted. For safety, soldiers always walk in pairs, but this afternoon I didn't have the customary battle buddy beside me.

Woman to woman, we stared at one another. From within the darkness behind her, I saw a shadow move, her fingers motioning me to come into her house. I recognized the universal gesture in a flash. My feet instantly became cemented to the hot sand beneath me; shock stopped me in my tracks. Why was she inviting a lone American soldier to go behind the walls of her home?

I didn't know what to do. I remembered the three soldiers who had been kidnapped and whose body parts were found strewn across the desert a week later in the Sunni Triangle. I knew Iraq was full of civilians and enemies. This was a guerilla war. Not knowing who was who had become part of the daily, grating fear inside my belly.

Should I trust this woman? She could be bait, luring me into an attack, where I'd be taken by the enemy hiding behind her door and never heard from again. I wasn't all that afraid of dying, but I was terrified of being raped and tortured. I knew the sorts of things people could do to you to make you wish for death, and as a woman, I had more to lose than my male soldiers, and I knew it. Looking around, I realized I had wandered away from the safety of my fellow soldiers and was all alone. Alarm bells of danger started to roar in my ears. My eyes started to sting with tears held back. I felt the pressure building inside me.

I could decide to protect myself or to take a risk and move toward this woman instead of away. I didn't know why she was inviting a soldier who had invaded her country and wore a gun into her home, but she was. In a split second, I knew I could either stick to the script or leave the safety of what I knew and plow into the rapids of the unknown without a life jacket. Was I going to trust someone I didn't already know was trustworthy, or was I going to play it safe?

My heart pounded. I didn't know whether she was safe. I didn't know whether she was a suicide bomber wrapped up in a grandmotherly smile or whether my name would be read the following morning at roll call from the list of soldiers killed. But even though everything in my training and survival instincts screamed at me to walk away, and fast, something undeniable drew me toward her. Something bigger was challenging my wartime survival instincts. Like a burning bush I couldn't ignore, her eyes locked on mine, and I knew I had a choice to make: to walk away or to accept the fireworks in my chest that were screaming at me not to miss this, to pay attention even if I didn't understand it. Inhaling hard, I felt my heart pump as if I were standing on the edge of the high dive.

Then I suddenly felt a flash of hope like summer lightning streaking across the night sky. Her invitation to choose hope over fear was the oxygen mask I didn't know I needed. The choice to put it on was mine alone. And I wasn't sure if I could do it.

Her invitation dared me to be human in the middle of an inhuman war. She dared me to believe in the stuff that my little-girl self had thought was possible: goodness in the middle of the most violent darkness. Her twinkling eyes dared me to believe that I had something extravagant to give instead of something priceless to protect. I could dare to love, even in the middle of a war, or I could settle for staying alive.

Practitioners of dangerous hope are found in the most unlikely places: Iraqis offering friendship to Americans; children grabbing hands of soldiers, believing they will hold them instead of harm them; a parent tying a bow into a child's hair, knowing a bomb or a bullet may go off that same day; and prayers of gratitude in the predawn morning of a gritty war. These are dangerous ways to hope in unlikely places.

This dangerous hope propelled me into the woman's home, and I've never been the same. Today, seventeen years later, I know that this woman changed my life forever. She interrupted my well-worn path of self-protection with an invitation of unearned trust. Despite my uniform announcing my status as an invader into her country, the nine-millimeter Beretta weapon strapped to my hip, and the battle rattle hanging off of me, she saw me. She saw a little girl, far away from home. No amount of military might or American superpower status could disguise my humanity.

That day, I didn't stare down at the sand and keep walking, ignoring her invitation. I walked through her doorway into the unknown. She laughed and wrapped her arms around me as she pulled me through the darkened hallway into the light of her living room, lined with bright-red rugs dotted with daughters, grandchildren, and embroidered cushions. I would drink tea on her family's rug, surrounded by her daughters and grandchildren, throughout my deployment. Her family would remind me of mine, and I would learn to laugh even when fear was eating away at my humanity.

* * *

Later I would listen as my new friend, Om Hassan, the one who had invited me into her home that day, retold how she had taken care of her children and grandchildren while her husband was gone as a soldier through the brutal minefield of the Iran-Iraq War. Om Hassan wasn't just my bridge of friendship into this village—she was the one who led the village through surviving. When neighbors are fighting each other, the situation is particularly deadly because of their proximity. When you share the same streets and the same schools, there's nowhere to be safe. I met Om Hassan in southern Iraq, a community largely made up of Shia Muslims whom Iraqi president Saddam Hussein a Sunni Muslim, feared and hated. He terrorized them into submission. The American invasion wasn't her first taste of violence.

Om Hassan held the family together while her husband was a POW in Iran and Saddam rained down terror on her village. I listened to tales of Saddam's government forbidding them from wearing shoes, to shame them as second-class citizens. The bottom of a shoe is considered dirty and unclean; pointing the bottom of your shoe at someone is an insult. To deny a person shoes is to make them unclean and disqualify them from worshipping with the community.

Fear couldn't dampen her relentless job as a mother, keeping her children alive. Every day, she searched for food and watered the possibility of their future. Through all the years, the chant of food and water and building a bridge to the future for her children drove her. When it came to staying alive and keeping her family alive, she was no amateur. She knew how to play this song well.

27

* * *

Fifteen years after I met Om Hassan, I would find myself sitting in my living room with my two toddler boys piled like puppies onto my lap in the afternoon sunshine. Then and there, I could finally see what she had done back in the war. She had dared to live out God's command to love our enemies, and her action had set me free in ways I hadn't understood. I could follow the thread of her unlikely friendship woven through my 397 days in war, a friendship that rescued me from my self and saved a part of me from breaking—because violence always breaks us, whether we are the one doling it out or are on the receiving end of it.

She chose to trust me, before I trusted her. She chose to honor my humanity before I acknowledged hers. She moved toward me before she knew if I was trustworthy. She chose to embrace my humanness before she knew what it would cost her. She accepted the risk of inviting an armed soldier into her home.

I'll never know why. But I'm eternally grateful for her offering me what I would later call an unlikely act of preemptive love. It's a love that jumps first, knowing it may be costly. It's love choosing to write a new story between people who see each other as enemies. She sneak-attacked me with preemptive love, and my life has never recovered.

Om Hassan is the reason I am trying to live without enemies today. She taught me how to live out my faith's call to love my enemies instead of hate them. Her self-sacrificing love changed my perspective, allowing me to see people I once feared as friends. She showed me what it looks like to follow the example of Jesus, who gave himself up for us while we were still his enemies.

She's the reason that my first identity is as a citizen of heaven instead of a citizen of my country. She's the reason I found what was worth living for and what I would gladly die for. I don't even know if she's alive today, but I'm fully alive because of her.

I want to thank her.

I want my sons to see her twinkling eyes and round cheeks. I want them to feel the hands that hugged their future mother when she was a scared twenty-three-year-old walking a tightrope of life and death, faith and fear, during war.

I want her to see the lives she's made possible by her creaky-door opening and brave invitation on that hot ordinary Wednesday afternoon. I want her to see my sons' love for Iraqi people, because she first loved me. I want her to hear their toddler laughter, because they live with a wholehearted, fully alive mama instead of a war-torn shell of quiet regret or enemy hate.

Her invitation to choose preemptive love over fear has blazed through my life like a wildfire and set my soul on fire—ignited to choose love instead of fear. It opened my eyes to see that when I choose the other, even if I lose, even if it costs me my life, I don't really lose. Because love never fails. And in the end, after everything ceases, love remains. Deciding what I will live for, no matter what, no matter where, and whatever the cost, is the freedom I was missing.

I've found the thing that can't rust, that can't be destroyed, and that can't be bought or taken away from me. There is a wider and longer table than I grew up believing was possible. Wide-eyed and grateful to be included in God's worldwide family, I look to the right and to the left. So many people that God crafted and loves are surrounding me.

Om Hassan gave me a lifeboat to leap from my self-protecting, self-serving life, and I let that old life go under the water and die. Without death, there can be no new life.

* * *

Three weeks after I met Om Hassan, my combat engineering unit was still working on digging a culvert in the village road. Getting to the village in the rainy season was next to impossible when the road washed out, cutting off the villagers from work and school. During that time, Om Hassan, as the matriarch of the village, introduced me to every house in the village on the winding dirt path. I'd spend my days being led into a house, drinking tea, and asking through broken Arabic and simple translation if anyone in the family had any medical needs. My medic pack was basic, but so is human relationship. A cleaned cut here or a Band-Aid there was all a pretense for getting close enough to look into the whites of each other's eyes and say, "I see you." Friendship is a song made as our shoulders rub together like violin strings putting a melody into the air around us.

Stepping into yet another mud-colored home on one of my visits, I ducked through the outside gate and escaped the harsh sunshine, my eyes adjusting to the shaded inner courtyard of the family home. Hard dirt formed a front yard expertly intertwining the mud and brush into a stately barrier for the clucking chickens that voiced their disapproval of my visit. Ducking under another doorway, I was welcomed with cheerful chatter. "Salaam alaikum" (Arabic for "peace be with you"), I crooned in my most Minnesota-nice voice, drizzled with the sweetness of maple syrup. It was the only greeting I hoped would put my hosts at ease while I was wearing my full battle rattle.

I lived in my flak vest and Kevlar helmet, with my gas mask and nine-millimeter Beretta gun strapped to my hip. Bandages, bullets, airways, and tourniquets dangled from my vest like ornaments on a Christmas tree. I wondered what I must have looked like to them. How could I communicate that, though I wore the uniform of the invading army and traveled in a Humvee crowned with a Mk 19 machine gun on top that could shred a body into spaghetti in under three seconds, I meant them no harm? Even I was confused by the paradox of this picture—confused because what I wore on the outside didn't match my growing belief in freedom instead of fear, in hope and shared humanity over cycles of violence.

Inside the home, a little girl's hand urgently pulled me to sit down. The darkened room shut out the fierce heat of the morning while my eyes strained to look through the dim shadows around me. A flock of children were scurrying around each other as I watched surprising pink curtains, nearly threadbare from wear, float across a tiny breeze in the window. A daring tangle of wires that sprouted from a bare electric wire hanging down into the room delivered electricity to a fridge and a lamp. The walls were covered with religious calendars on which a holy man wearing a permanent frown perched on top of the months of the year. I sat on a rug whose riotous reds chased bright yellows around bursts of turquoise licking at my feet. The Bible story of Joseph's many-colored coat, which I had heard over and over in the damp church basement of my childhood, suddenly came alive when I saw the many-colored rug beneath me.

Women entered the room, carrying tea on platters as big as a sled. Children tumbled into the room and curled up on each side of me. This unspoken routine occurred in each house I visited. For my hosts, hospitality wasn't a hollow display of politeness, but a sacrificial practice of their Muslim faith. Making others more important than themselves showed honor to God and humility to strangers. Serving others, whether or not they have food to spare, is a foundation of their faith.

The grandmother, Om Hassan, introduced me to the lady of the house while simultaneously scolding the unrelenting stream of children that flooded into the house beside me with wild hair and sand-caked feet. We shook hands, and I tried to stretch out my sparse Arabic, pulling a conversation out of the tiny amount of Arabic words I knew. I would point to my medic bag and ask if anyone was sick. Someone always knew more English than I knew in Arabic and would interpret my pointing and smiling into symptoms and needs. Sometimes it was Band-Aids or lotion for irritated skin; always it included drops to soothe eyes from the sandpaper-like wind that scraped the whites of eyes during sandstorms.

At each house we went to, family members with ailments would be paraded up to me after the tea, pleasantries, and routine scolding of the unruly kids. After the third house, I started to become curious about the matriarch of the village, Om Hassan. Why was she in every family photo I was shown at each new house? And why did each of the women have her wide smile and laughing eyes? Eventually, I realized that the ties that bound together this baker's dozen homes on this dusty hilltop were family ties. Each home I entered was the home of one of Om Hassan's daughters or daughters-in-law.

Her husband, who should have been the village elder, had been taken during the Iran-Iraq War. Everyone spoke of him as though he were alive, even though it had been over a decade since the war. Hope seemed to sustain this village like the hot cups of tea we drank throughout the harshest parts of the day. In his absence, Om Hassan was the champion of this village.

After that first day in which I stepped into Om Hassan's house, another soldier got assigned to accompany me as I went from house to house in the village, offering medical attention. Before long, being the "medic guard" became a preferred duty in the daily rotation. For most soldiers, it would be their only contact with Iraqis.

My company of combat engineers continued to rebuild the road to the village while I ducked into houses and offered medical care and friendship, day after day. The rhythm of these days revived a sense of hope for me as I sat with mothers and children who brought back into focus who I was, reminding me of our shared humanity and the God who delights in us all.

* * *

The fear and violence of war had all but darkened my vision, keeping me from seeing people as more than "other" and making me defensive of even those within my own unit. Every morning, I tamped down the clawing fear in my belly that I was in real danger—and not just due to the enemies outside of our tent camp. I had already heard of more female soldiers being sexually assaulted by their fellow soldiers than attacked by the enemy. Walking to the portable toilet at night alone had already proved dangerous to one female soldier in my tent city. And while we weren't able to buy toothbrushes because our camp was still a remote and isolated group of tents in the desert, a webcam was found hidden in the female showers.

If an enemy soldier raped an American soldier, the order would be to shoot first and ask questions later. But when I heard the announcement that a female soldier in our tent city who had been jogging in broad daylight was raped by a soldier, the order was not to shoot or bring our weapons with us to jog. The order was to run in pairs.

Rape is never about lust; it's about power and putting people in their place. Rape has been part of war long before women served in the military. It's part of a violent tradition of hazing—men raping and pillaging men, the ultimate humiliation of putting another person in their place by using their own body as a weapon against them.

And this is why female soldiers of lower rank, like me, are especially vulnerable. The chain of command makes it difficult and dangerous to report abuse by higher-ranking male soldiers.

Basic training taught me not only how to be an infantry foot soldier, but also that I would be preyed upon by those in power over me. My basic training class was one of the first to be integrated by an order of Congress. In fact, the US military is still working toward full gender integration. The drill sergeants overseeing the first integrated basic training cycles were so angry they had to share the honor of soldiering with women that they sexually assaulted so many that the yearlong program had to be halted soon after I graduated.

I was asked to give the invocation prayer that opens the graduation ceremony. My family didn't come to see me graduate. I was almost glad they didn't come to see the place that had taught me things I didn't want to know.

When I graduated basic training, a drill sergeant drove me to the airport in a two-and-a-half-ton pickup truck. He sat in the front cab, and I sat on top of my green duffle bag in the bed of the truck in the rain for the duration of the hour-long drive from Fort Leonard Wood in Missouri to the airport. When the truck stopped at the curb, I jumped down, relieved to be so close to getting back home. I heaved my duffle onto my back and was surprised to feel a tap on my shoulder. This drill sergeant had yelled in my face for twelve straight weeks, so I took a deep breath and waited for his last barrage of Army-appointed insults. "You're a good soldier," he said in his trademark Oklahoma drawl as he leaned toward me. "They are going to try to take things from you. Don't let them." And then he turned on his heel with a crisp about face, and all I saw were his camouflaged shoulders and black combat boots walking away from me. His words were suspended in the air in front of me. I didn't know if he knew his fellow drill sergeant had tried pinning me against the wall in our basic training bay late at night, initiating me into the military tradition of being sexually preyed upon by those in power over you. But I know that he saw me, an eighteen-year-old woman, and was telling me to prepare myself because defending myself against those wearing my same uniform would be my first battle, a battle I would need to be on alert for as long as I wore the uniform.

I would always have two front lines, the enemy in front of me and the violence in the trench next to me. I wasn't safe anywhere. Later I would find out that in a survey, over half of all female soldiers deployed to Iraq or Afghanistan would say they had been sexually assaulted during their deployment. My service and loyalty to the flag couldn't protect me from the violence that happens in the ranks; this is what my drill sergeant knew.

These experiences have changed me forever. The people I saw as my enemy were inviting me in for tea, while some of my fellow soldiers were using the cover of our uniform to commit crimes like rape and torture. The flag, country, and military I'd grown up worshipping weren't so pure and honorable after all. And the people who were supposed to be my enemies were instead welcoming me into their homes. I thought we were the "good guys," but the story was so much more complicated, and I couldn't look away.

5

Life, Limb, or Eyesight

I looked at my hands to see if I was the same person now I was free. There was such glory over everything. The sun came up like gold through the trees and I felt like I was in heaven.
—Harriet Tubman, *Harriet, the Moses of her People*

Om Hassan, the matriarch of the village called Awaijah who had befriended me and challenged me to accept her invitation to enter her home, had opened doors into more homes than I could count. I fell into a daily rhythm of doing my medic rounds, visiting the village families. I would treat swollen ears on a little girl, clean an infected foot, and soothe a buffet of respiratory and skin ailments resulting from the constant dust in the air and the beating sun on the skin. We built trust one laugh and one story at a time. As I grew accustomed to the pace and flavor of village life, I felt a sliver of home that I hadn't felt since putting my boots into the russet-colored sand.

During one of these visits, while we were surrounded by more mothers and children than usual, Om Hassan leaned over with an unusually serious look in her eye. We still communicated mostly

37

through hand gestures and facial expressions, which covered most of the basics, and some English dotted with my sprouting Arabic. So it sent a message when, instead of smiling as we drank our tea, shoulders nestling into the shared space as they rubbed between us, she locked her eyes on mine and held on. Before someone tells you bad news, the air crystalizes, and you know it before they speak. The air turned heavy, and her expression told me a storm was coming, and I needed to brace myself for it. Taking a deep breath in, I slowly nodded my head to indicate that she had my attention. Problems here are about life and death, and entering their home meant I had a front-row seat to the struggle and pain of surviving.

Om Hassan's daughter settled on her right, solemnly handing her a tiny bundle of bright white cloth. Peeking out from the bundle was an impossibly tiny wisp of baby hair. As Om Hassan carefully handed me this swaddled bundle, I could see that the wisp of wild black hair was framing the face of a baby with glassy dull eyes. An icy shiver ran down my spine as he was passed toward my outstretched arms. Something was deadly wrong with this baby.

"Muhammad," his mother whispered to me while tears filled her eyes to the brim, threatening to spill down her cheeks. I knew that once I cradled this baby in my arms, there was no going back, at least not for me. When I held him in my arms, I wouldn't be able to disentangle myself from him.

My hands barely registered his birdlike weight as I cradled Baby Muhammad in my arms. "Three months," his mother choked out, holding her three fingers up in the air like a flag of surrender. No three-month-old baby should be mistaken for a newborn. His low weight was the proof that his life was dangling by a string, hovering in front of his mother's watchful eyes. The pain etched into each face circling this baby illustrated their fear: this baby they loved was losing an unseen battle. Since the invasion, clean water had been hard to come by. Muhammad's mother gestured to explain that he had been suffering from diarrhea for weeks. When she couldn't find formula for him, he would eat only water, and the diarrhea would get worse.

I carefully and slowly laid him on the floor and began to unwrap his swaddled body like a Christmas gift. Most babies cry when their warm, snug blankets are taken away. Not this baby. His silence filled the room as his bare body lay on the rug in front of my knees. He didn't fuss, and the limpness of his head lolling to the side rang alarm bells in my medical brain. The room filled up with a tense, pregnant pause, and I knew my reaction to this child would either offer hope to his family or terrify them. I steeled my face, praying it was a billboard of calm instead of revealing the panic beginning to pump through my veins. Looking at the mother, I pushed my cheeks into a serious half smile and gave her a nod of reassurance. Tears running down her face, her head dipped in the slightest nod to continue.

I moved the blanket away to reveal skeleton bones where a round baby should have been. Before being deployed to the war in Iraq, I had worked in the oncology and hospice ward at the hospital, bearing witness to patients' last moments on earth. Being a hospice nurse left me with an awareness of the closeness of life and death in a room, fighting within the same body. Muhammad's body told me the story of the fight for life his body had been losing. He was so malnourished that where I expected to find round baby cheeks, I found sunken eyes. Where I expected to find chubby arms and legs, I felt only the weight of his bones. This three-month-old baby couldn't have weighed more than a premature baby born weeks too soon.

I leaned over him, willing him to look at me or to have a strong pulse or deceptively strong breathing. As I laid my hand on his frail chest, waiting to feel his breath raise my hand, I leaned over and put

39

my cheek next to his pale rosebud lips, hoping to feel the soft breeze of his exhalation tickle my cheek. His chest sagged like a worn-out party balloon, inflating just enough to register on my palm while his breath limped across my cheek in short, fleeting, and unsteady puffs. Laying my adult-sized stethoscope on his miniature chest felt dangerous, like smothering a fire with too big of a log. His heart moved to an unsteady beat, rather than the lub-dub rhythm I had hoped to hear. The silence in the room kept pressing in on my chest, making sweat stream down the sides of my face. The desperate prayers and hope over this baby weighed heavily on my twenty-three-year-old shoulders.

Even under that heavy weight, I got lost in the magic of this baby—his rippling tawny skin, his ebony eyelashes brushing against his cheek, and his curly hair that reminded me of a Dr. Seuss character. He was stunning. Forcing myself back to the examination, I held out one last hope for a sign of optimism about this boy's future. I checked the place where his body ought to hold stores of fat to make it through sickness. A baby's bum, so round and cute, is also practical. Brown fat stored there is a baby's savings account against hard times like sickness or hunger. It's the last defense for a baby. Lifting his fragile frame up into my arms, I exhaled, whispered a desperate prayer, and then turned him over. Instead of a bottom shaped like an ice-cream scoop, he had a flat board where his bottom should have been. It looked like his back just kept going down to his legs, uninterrupted by a baby bottom, as if someone had forgotten that he needed some cushion to sit down on.

Fear finally broke to the surface, like a diver coming up for air. I didn't know if this baby would live another week or even another twenty-four hours. Babies are unpredictable. They are fragile; that's why we hold them close to our chest and never let them down for the first two years. They are sprinters, not marathon runners. They can't handle being sick for more than short bursts. But the appearance of Baby Muhammad's skeletal limbs and bum told me that his body had already spent the extra fat it once had. There wasn't much left for his body to fight with.

Being a combat medic gave me a different set of rules than other soldiers to follow. When I graduated from basic training, I was battle trained as an infantry soldier. Every soldier's primary job is to be able to lead a ground attack and kill accurately at up to three hundred yards with an M16 automatic rifle. The first two weeks of basic training are about establishing this skill. If you don't master it, they have no use for you and will cut you loose, send you home. No more wasted time or money will be invested in training you. First things first. Shoot to kill.

After basic, I trained as a combat medic, and I graduated with a new standing order. I no longer carried an M16 rifle to shoot to kill. I carried a medic bag that took up my entire back, and a small pistol, a nine-millimeter Beretta sidearm, strapped to my thigh. No longer was my order to kill, but to protect life on the battlefield at all cost. The Beretta wasn't much firepower; it was just enough to protect me or my patient. My change in weapon reflected my change in purpose. My first general order was to protect the life, limb, or eyesight of every person on the battlefield, regardless of what side they were on. I was fighting on the side of life.

The highest-ranking soldier on the battlefield makes the commanding decisions. The only exception is that if life, limb, or eyesight is in danger, then a lowly medic can overrule the command of a full-bird colonel. Medics are trained to save lives, while colonels are trained to win battles. When lives are on the line, a medic takes charge. To send an Iraqi, even an infant, to a US military hospital was a big deal; for it to be possible, the rules say that life, limb, or eyesight must be in immediate danger.

If I left this dehydrated, limp baby in the house, I wasn't sure he would be alive when I came back the next day. Baby Muhammad's unsteady breaths didn't give me much confidence. Three-month-olds aren't fighters yet. They are supposed to be protected in all ways imaginable—shielded from the risk of even a rogue fingernail scratching his delicate new skin or from the chill of a cool breeze. Clearly, his life was in immediate danger.

That was how I could justify my decision to others, but what motivated me was something much deeper. Babies are life and hope all wrapped up in the most defenseless and stunning package. This family passed Baby Muhammad around like he was made of spun sugar and moonbeams. While the war raged, this baby brought smiles and laughter to weary mothers and desperate fathers. This family, snuggled around him, needed him to stay—to stay alive and offer them a reason to hope for a future in which they would survive and their children would thrive.

And I needed him to stay. Holding this baby in my arms woke me up. He flooded me with a fierce hope. War had clouded out the everyday miracles and made me suspicious of everything good. Baby Muhammad ignited a joy I had thought was gone—one of the first casualties of this war. Good things like the magic of an elongated baby yawn and the sweet competition between siblings vying to rock a baby still existed, and one of the best of these things was struggling to breathe in my camouflaged arms. Surrounded by weapons and two groups trying to kill each other, I needed to see that life could prevail over death. Baby Muhammad needed to stay alive. He needed a chance, and that wouldn't be possible if I left him in the village.

I knew my mission. Even if it would cost me the safety of

invisibility, a loss of rank, or disciplinary action, I was going to fight for his life. I couldn't stop much of the dying around me, but I could stop Baby Muhammad's death—if his body held on for just a little while longer.

Nestling Baby Muhammad back into his mother's arms, I gathered my medic bag, threw on my Kevlar helmet, and rushed out the house, calling back over my shoulder that I would be back soon. The next hour, I stood in front of every sergeant I knew, pleading Baby Muhammad's case. One laughed at me, saying, "We aren't here to help the ragheads." Another barked, "Go away! This is not my problem." Standing in front of each person in power, I'd repeat quietly, "This baby's life is in danger, and when life, limb, or eyesight is in danger, as a medic, I'm required to take any and all means necessary to save that life." My cheeks burned red, and my knees knocked every time I was dismissed, but the words "I'm not going to let him die" kept running through my head, pounding out a quickening drumbeat, because I didn't know how much time Baby Muhammad had.

Finally, I found myself staring into the eyes of the commanding colonel of the Air Force tent hospital. I dug my desert-crusted boots deeper into the hot sand underneath me. That moment was Baby Muhammad's last chance. This colonel was the last person who could give permission to bring Muhammad into our camp for medical care. I knew how this was going to go. I expected to get an earful and be sent away with a shouted "Dismissed!" But I couldn't walk away, because a life was suspended in the air, struggling to take a breath in his mother's arms in a village down the road, where I'd left twenty anxious faces.

"Why should I care about a civilian's baby while we are fighting an enemy we can't even find?" he barked through clenched teeth, face twitching around his mouth. The yelling stopped. Leaning over my five-foot frame and down into my face, he grunted, "Dismissed."

This was when I was supposed to scurry out of the room, holding my butt that he had just chewed in both hands. Silently, with my hands clenched behind my back, boots twelve inches apart, and chin frozen at a ninety-degree angle, I stayed locked into the military position of parade rest, as if I were carved out of granite. Eyes straight ahead, I didn't move an inch. This Air Force colonel didn't know I was Army. I had been pinned to walls with hard hands and felt hot breath hissing in my ear since basic training had initiated me into the military. His berating me was a G-rated movie compared with what I'd experienced. His words made my knees tremble, but they couldn't touch me. I was braced for the attack and recognized the weapon of intimidation he used.

I remembered the flicker of life I had seen in Baby Muhammad's eyes—the same spark of magic that had made me marvel at every single baby I'd ever held while I was growing up. Babies were like saltwater taffy, stretching their impossible hope between themselves and anyone within arm's length. Their stickiness caught us and connected us to each other and to them. Muhammad needed to live, because if he died, if he joined all the death that this war had piled up already, there wouldn't be a container in which we could carry our grief. Babies shouldn't die, no matter what, no matter where.

Even though every muscle in my body told me to nod and walk away from this colonel, I kept standing in the same spot, digging into something I couldn't disentangle myself from. Backing down wasn't an option anymore; staying quiet wasn't something I could do. All babies are worth fighting for.

The colonel at the Air Force tent hospital had said no to my bringing the baby in to be treated by his team. Yet the authority

44

of my medic code to act when life, limb, or eyesight was in danger superseded his authority to say no. His face turned red, and his lips turned tight as he realized that this nobody of a female Army medic, at five feet nothing, was challenging his direct order instead of walking out the door. I invoked my medic code, which required him to authorize me to bring in Baby Muhammad to be treated. He had no choice but to agree, so his team said they would be standing by.

Later, when we ducked into the tent hospital and found it deserted except for the four-person trauma team playing cribbage, I couldn't help but wonder what he had been busy with when he was arguing about allowing Baby Muhammad to be treated.

* * *

Bringing an Iraqi through three different Army checkpoints on our way back to camp promised to be as difficult as it is to try flossing your teeth with cotton candy—nearly impossible. It wasn't going to work; this was a guerilla war waged with hidden improvised explosive devices, bombs camouflaged as baby diapers, roads riddled with hidden snipers, and suicide bombers. Checkpoints were the first and only real line of defense. Bringing into a checkpoint an elderly Iraqi grandma covered in a head-to-toe black robe that could hide a microwave oven would set off every alarm bell. Om Hassan didn't stand a chance of making it through the scrutiny of the checkpoint.

We soldiers couldn't admit to the fear we woke up with every day in war, so the language many soldiers spoke was a mix of anger and bravado. Like a boxer preparing to get into the ring, we used anger to feed the fight in us when we prepared to face unknown dangers we couldn't fend off. President Bush may have said liberating the Iraqi people from Saddam Hussein's tyranny was the goal, but he

45

sent in the Army, not the Peace Corps. We are trained to fight, not humanitarians, and it showed in the attitudes of the soldiers manning the checkpoints.

To save Baby Muhammad under these circumstances, we needed to hurry, and these checkpoints were a maze of red tape. "Life, limb, or eyesight" was my only weapon to get through the checkpoints. I couldn't tell my friend Om Hassan that no one wanted her inside the camp. I couldn't tell her that Baby Muhammad had a better chance of getting through the checkpoints without his grandma who loved him. Her skin color, what she wore, and her religion screamed "enemy" at best or "suicide bomber" at the worst.

At the same time, I knew I couldn't take this baby away from this village, with the chance of him dying on my hands, without her. If I, as an American soldier, took this village's beautiful baby boy to the hospital alive and returned with him dead, there would be no way to make it OK. Bridging the gulf of trust and grief seemed like a bridge stocked with gunpowder laced with a fuse, ready to blow with one misstep. If the worst happened, there could be a riot. Om Hassan was the biggest stumbling block to getting Muhammad to the hospital, yet she also was my safety net. She believed in my intention to help her grandson and had the standing in the village to lead them through the sorrow of losing Baby Muhammad if he didn't make it back alive. I needed her in so many more ways than I knew. Her steely resolve made me stand up straighter, like iron fortifying my spine, while her laughter reminded me that I was still human.

When I brought Om Hassan out to the two-and-a-half-ton truck that would bring Baby Muhammad back to camp, I exchanged a furtive glance with the soldier who was going to drive. His eyes locked on mine, after which we both looked up at the door of the truck above my head and then down at Om Hassan. The tires of this truck are so big that you have to climb a metal ladder to get in. Neither of us knew how a grandmother draped in six yards of billowing black fabric would be able to make it up. I was holding Muhammad while the driver of the truck stood kicking dirt with his combat boots, unsure of where he should put his hands to help Om Hassan up into the truck. While we tried to hatch a plan that would be appropriate across cultural norms, she swung herself up into the truck. By the time I realized what had just happened, I was looking up at her smiling face. She was already getting situated in the truck and nodding for me to get a move on and hand up the baby. The driver and I traded bewildered shoulder shrugs. We knew enough to recognize when a problem had been solved and the job was done. She had got it done.

Om Hassan sat by the door, and I snuggled Baby Muhammad into the crook of my camouflaged arm while sitting in the middle of the truck on top of the radio and communication equipment. We were in an emergency, but I still wanted to buffer her from sitting next to a male who wasn't a relative. Settled in, the driver kicked the engine into gear, and we started to roll out.

All three of us knew that this baby had a limited number of breaths left in him and that our entrance through three checkpoints wasn't guaranteed. I couldn't think, and I couldn't stop breathing fast. We were on the road, heading toward the camp hospital, but we were still so far away from knowing whether Muhammad would be OK. "Please let him live, God," I prayed in a whisper. My words were drowned out by the roar of the diesel engine as the truck rolled down the road toward our first checkpoint.

I held Baby Muhammad up onto my chest, hoping the beat of my heart would encourage his to beat along with mine. My breath started to match Muhammad's rapid, shallow gasps for air. His small tummy jerked down, straining to pull down his diaphragm, filling his tiny lungs with oxygen. "Don't stop breathing, don't stop breathing," I pleaded out loud to him. "Please don't stop breathing, Muhammad. Please stay with us. I know it's so hard, but please don't quit."

I needed him to keep fighting. With the din of the truck and the screaming brakes, I feared his tiny body would be quietly still by the time we arrived but I wouldn't notice until we stopped, too late. "We've come so far," I pleaded, "please stay with us." I knew something in me would break if I watched him die. If I brought him back dead and had to witness the grief of my friends in the village, something in me would die, too. Deep love requires deep grief. The cost is high; the reward is great. He was a prized possession in his family—and to me. Losing him alongside of them would be devastating.

Five miles from the village, we hit the first checkpoint. It was a small barricade manned by a few soldiers stopping traffic outside the next small village. Slowing down, we waited in the line of vehicles inching to the barricade. As the soldier leaned in to check us, he raised his eyebrows when he saw Om Hassan filling up the passenger seat next to me, covered in black from head to toe. This would be our first test. All I had was a verbal authorization to plead my case. The soldier at the checkpoint could say no and turn us back. After staring at me long and hard, he looked back over his shoulder to his sergeant. Then he shrugged his shoulders and waved us through. Exhaling with relief, Om Hassan and I looked at each other and grinned. We were on our way.

The first two checkpoints were in the outskirts of towns, low security for local villages. The last, getting into an American camp, would be the real test.

I was holding my breath, fear clamping down on my rib cage,

making it hard to breathe, when we rolled into the last checkpoint—the most guarded checkpoint, right before the gate admitting us entry into camp. Inside, over a thousand soldiers were safe behind rolls of razor wire and guards. I pushed away thoughts of the gate guard on duty sending us back after we had been so close. I was desperate for my fellow soldiers to see Om Hassan as I did—to let them know that she saw them as people far from home, instead of only by the uniforms they wore. I couldn't bring them to her house for tea, where she would show them the storied hospitality of the Middle East. I couldn't translate her beautiful heart to them in thirty seconds at a checkpoint. Instead, I watched Muhammad's tiny chest work hard to suck air in and push it out, and I sang to him, "Little bird, little bird, please keep breathing." His breathing reminded me of the spring hummingbirds in Minnesota and the furious beating of their wings. "Please baby," I whispered, "keep your heart beating. We need you." I was so focused on staring at his face that I didn't realize at first that the truck had started moving again. We were through. The guards had waved us in. We were finally in camp and approaching the camp hospital.

The colonel's trauma team rushed through the green tent's zippered door and scooped Muhammad out of my arms. With trauma-trained efficiency, they whisked him onto a waiting white gurney. Three people stood around it, blue rubber gloves raised in the air, gowned up over desert fatigues with brown combat boots peeking out underneath. The glare of the spotlight shining onto the middle of the gurney highlighted Baby Muhammad's birdlike limbs and blue veins under his skin.

Om Hassan and I sat in the darkened tent hallway. Waves of air conditioning rolled across our sweat-soaked shoulders, cooling the metal folding chairs we sat in. Neither of us was accustomed to air conditioning. After the trek to get here, the coolness was soothing. Behind us and on the other side of a thin fabric divider, we could hear the trauma team start working on Baby Muhammad. "Where's the blood?" I heard an incredulous male voice ask from the operating room behind me. It was battlefield humor, always in bad taste and never funny. But I knew what he meant. The Air Force rotated their soldiers into this tent hospital for voluntary three-month deployments. They never leave the camp or go outside the protection of the wire, because it's not their job. Om Hassan and her grandson might be the only Iraqis they would ever see. The soldier making the wisecrack about blood probably had at some point imagined the war stories he would tell his friends back home, and those stories were most likely *not* about waiting around, playing cribbage inside an air-conditioned tent, and saving a baby from a deadly case of dehydration.

"Medic!" someone bellowed through the small space. Scrambling up from the metal chair, I went to answer the colonel's command. Bending down to make his point, he repeated what I had heard through the curtain. He couldn't believe I'd invoked "life, limb, or eyesight" for a child who "wasn't bloody enough." But the whole time he was dressing me down, I felt hope bursting inside of me. He wasn't telling me Muhammad was dying, which meant the baby might have a shot at surviving after all.

As I stood at parade rest, wearing the neutral stone face that lower-ranking soldiers perfect, hope started to bubble up inside me. Thoughts of "He's going to live! He's actually going to live!" bounced around in my heart as the colonel talked at me. I didn't care about this colonel's criticism over my "field decision-making," because he and I both knew our places. He'd never stepped out into the desert dust, where the snipers take potshots at you, or witnessed

50

the desperation of the Iraqi people we were here to liberate, because his place was saving lives in the hospital. He went from his air-conditioned tent clinic to his air-conditioned chow hall. I respected his place, even if he didn't respect mine. "Dismissed" he barked, but as he turned away from me, he said over his shoulder as an afterthought, "He was so dehydrated that he wouldn't have made it another twelve hours." Those words were the best news of my life. Baby Muhammad was going to live and not die. He was going to breathe and breathe again.

They saved his tiny life. Weaving tiny tubes into his body in an effort that took all day, they delicately pumped fluid and rehydrated him until his shrunken skin turned baby plump again, giving his heart back the fluid it needed to pump throughout his body, oxygenating him until the bluish tinge on his lips turned rosebud red.

I ran back to tell Om Hassan the news. As I turned the corner and looked into the room, I saw her sitting in a metal folding chair, nose deep into an issue of *O, the Oprah Magazine,* whose cover was plastered with teasers for fashion and Thanksgiving turkey recipes. I skidded to a halt and soaked in this picture of a concerned woman sitting in a doctor's office with her nose deep into a magazine while she waits. Even in the middle of war, familiar moments sneak up on you, reminding you that people are people and that bringing a sick grandbaby to the hospital is an experience the world over. Guns, camouflage, and black modesty robes can't disguise the humanity of us all. In that moment, my Iraqi grandma friend had become every mother I knew.

I hurriedly told her the good news. Muhammad was stable, breathing well, and would have to stay until his tiny veins had received all the rehydration his body needed. I left out the colonel's closing remarks, although they still echoed in my mind: "He'd be dead by tomorrow if he didn't get rehydration therapy." She didn't need to know what a close call it had been; all she needed to know was that her grandbaby had life in him right now—that she had saved his life.

Near dusk, I stepped out of the tent clinic. As I breathed in the scorching desert air, thankfulness felt like a blanket wrapped around my shoulders. A flicker of hope seeped into my war-weary bones. Something good had happened that day, and I was part of it. Not only had I avoided the bullets and potholes and IEDs, but something miraculous and good had happened. Tears slid down my cheeks in the fading light, and gratefulness washed over me. I had seen life stamp out death. Muhammad's life had been snatched back from death's cold grip, and I knew it. His body's fight had almost ended this day, but it didn't.

The night sky over the desert was painted inky black with white stars suspended above so bright against the dark that they felt touchable. I exhaled the tension and fear I had been holding inside since I walked through the village that morning and held Baby Muhammad's sick body in my arms.

I wanted to lean into the joy of this incredible day—to squeeze every last drop of goodness out of this moment until my soul was dripping with its stickiness. But I didn't know if I could. If I allowed myself to feel these things, would I be able to wake up tomorrow morning and do my job? Until now, I'd survived in this war zone by cutting off my emotions. I armored up not just by putting on my bulletproof vest but also by putting on blinders to shut out what war feels like, what it costs the soul, what I saw, and who I saw doing it. If I let myself feel, I didn't know if I would survive.

After only three months in the war, the person I had been when we arrived didn't exist anymore. She was gone. I didn't know who I was now, but I did know I should scoop up joy when it happens. The stars glowed above me, and I wrapped myself in the wild beauty of Baby Muhammad.

* * *

Later, when we traveled out of camp back to the village, Om Hassan cradled Muhammad as if he was her gold trophy. The triumphant feeling in the truck dusted everything we passed—the roadside chicken stand, the sunset, the herd of sheep blocking half the road on their way home for the night—with Hollywood-like glitter. As we passed the familiar dirt roads, with the evening breeze whipping across my dusty face, everything I saw took on a new intensity. I had never realized how many different hues are contained in the color brown or how a sunset across the desert can illuminate the tan terrain into a rainbow of color. Something miraculous had happened that day, and even the surrounding landscape seemed to know it.

My mind was full of joyful, hopeful thoughts. In a few more miles, the whole village would know the good news, too. Every month, I'd bring a fresh supply of baby formula to the village, mailed to me from back home. As long as Muhammad's family made sure the water was boiled before it was mixed with the formula, they could keep the diarrhea and dehydration at bay.

As the truck slowed down to make the hard right turn off of the main road onto Awaijah's dirt path, Om Hassan and I looked at each other. When we had left the village in the morning, desperation had knit us together, and fear had painted our faces. Returning to the village in the evening, we couldn't stop smiling at each other and couldn't stop touching Muhammad's rehydrated and plump cheek. Cooing over this baby felt like fawning over a flicker of life, a spark of hope that if we were gentle enough, if we believed hard enough, we could coax that spark into a flame so big that Muhammad's whole family, all his siblings could run toward the hope of a bright future together. Against the dark backdrop of war, this flicker of hope lit up like a wildfire at night. Together, we felt the warmth of this unlikely hope.

The truck heaved up the hill to the row of dwellings lining the rise of the hilltop, backlit by the last streaks of sunlight. The burr of the engine, like the bell on an ice-cream truck, called the herd of children out to us. Soon we were surrounded by a parade of chattering, gleeful escorts. When the truck stopped in front of Baby Muhammad's house, amidst the buzz of energy, Om Hassan placed Muhammad in my arms, so she could make the climb down out of the truck. As she placed his body, still light as a feather, into my waiting arms, her magnetic eyes caught mine, and she whispered, "Shukran," which is Arabic for thank you.

"No," I said, stumbling over my words; I needed to thank her.

On the ground, she expertly herded the bouncing children and directed the order of revelry and passing of information. Hospitality would come first, in the form of tea, and then the adventure of the day would be told.

Shoulder to shoulder, we sat cross-legged in the main room on top of the brightly colored rug. Tea was passed into waiting hands as the hum of excitement continued to build. Everyone watched as Om Hassan drank her tea. She was lucky I didn't know more Arabic, or I would have broken decorum by blurting out how Muhammad had barely made it through the checkpoints, describing the colonel's verbal tirade even as he saved Muhammad's life, and explaining how strong Muhammad had been to come back from death's grip.

Finally, Om Hassan rested her thimble-sized tea glass down onto its saucer, signaling that it was time to retell the story. Her shoulders pushed back, straightening her weary back as she started to speak. I'll never know exactly what she said, but the room tumbled into squeals of delight, clapping, and women crying with joy. Baby Muhammad was passed around to each person in the room—each auntie, each uncle grabbed him to their chest and prayed and thanked God for his life.

Seeing this family's joy was like balm to my heart. Sitting quietly, I soaked it in—the impossibility of what had happened that day. This room had been deathly quiet twelve hours earlier, when I sat in the same place, holding Muhammad's limp body. Now the baby had light in his eyes, sustenance in his body, fluid pumping through his veins. His eyes, bright and curious, stared at us from under a forest of dark eyelashes.

As I sat in my own thoughts, soaking in this family's joy, three little girls descended on me, crawling into my lap and embracing me. Here I was, sitting in my army fatigues and battle rattle, far away from home yet feeling more welcomed than I ever had before.

* * *

When I left that night, I was broken open. My preconceived notions of who is family and who I have been told to view as "other" had disintegrated. I knew love, and I knew what family feels like, and in this small house in the middle of Iraq, I was wrapped up in both.

Putting people into categories and boxes is a quick way to move through the world—maybe even a smart, self-protective way. But it isn't truth, and that evening I had seen a new, more expansive vision.

There's no such thing as a good guy or a bad guy. We are all people, and we have the capacity to do good or to do harm. Each of us, with our words and actions, can either build someone else up or break someone's world in half. And every single day, we each have to get up in the morning and make the choice of which one we will do that day. Every single day.

I saw what Om Hassan chose. I saw her choose to build me up before she knew if I would break her world in half. I was armed and had all the power to hurt her and break the world of the village that relied on her leadership. But she got up that morning and chose to build instead of break.

She broke my small box in which I had categorized her as an enemy. That day in the village when she dared to open her door and invite me, a stranger, into her home made all the difference.

And I'm so glad she did.

6

Christmas Eve Miracle

To lose the earth you know, for greater knowing; to lose the life you have for greater life; to leave the friends you loved, for greater loving; to find a land more kind than home, more large than earth.
—Thomas Wolfe, *You Can't Go Home Again*

My fingers throbbed from the cold. I'd never have believed it if someone had told me the suffocating heat would end. But then the heat disappeared overnight and was replaced by a wet, bone-chilling cold that ran you over like a freight train. The cold felt as sharp as January in Minnesota. Iraq was a landscape of extremes. Each new month marched in with a new challenge, and now it was Christmas Eve.

I huddled around the exhaust pipe of the running Humvee, holding my fingers toward the sparse heat that the engine gave off. It felt so good that I had to keep myself from wrapping my fingers around the pipe and burning them. This isn't where I thought I'd be on Christmas. It was so unbearably cold and so far from the traditions of home I remembered from my childhood: piling into winter coats over red and green crushed-velvet dresses, standing close together in the darkened church sanctuary lit only by candles, and singing "Silent Night." Instead, I was waiting for the day's mission to end, so we could return to the safety of camp. To be caught outside camp after dark was like leaving your car door unlocked and the keys in the ignition; it was tempting fate, literally risking an ambush or giving a sniper an easy last shot of the day. I wanted a drink and then to eat and fall asleep, stretched out on my green cot under the yellow tent ceiling, trying not to think about having to get up and do it all over again.

"Let's roll," the sergeant bellowed. Prying my hands away from the delicious source of warmth, I pushed myself away and climbed up into the Humvee. The sun had disappeared, darkening the edges of the desert into a golden rim. "We have to get back inside camp," my head kept chanting. "It's not safe to be out after dark." No one wanted anyone to die. On this night of all nights, it felt more urgent than ever that no one should die, and the longer we stayed outside the safety of the wire surrounding camp, the greater the chance of that happening. I mounted up, and we turned toward camp. The mission was finished for the day—now it was time to get back inside the wire to safety. All I could do was cross my fingers and pray a little prayer that we wouldn't be surprised by a well-hidden IED or well-placed sniper fire.

As we bumped along through the fear and darkness, it didn't feel like Christmas. I could hardly remember what it was like to be a little girl who sang with conviction, "The weary world rejoices." I certainly felt weary, but I wasn't rejoicing, and neither were the Iraqis we were here to liberate. One dictator had been toppled, and now they were under the control of a variety of foreign soldiers who didn't speak their language and pointed M16s at them daily. None of us were free. Soldiers in battle rattle every day, not knowing who the enemy was or if there was an enemy, weren't free either. Civilians weren't free from the fear of the foreign soldiers marching through their streets with no common language or trust. We didn't seem to be making any progress. In a year or two, this stalemate would reach President Bush. Advisers quietly told him what the US soldiers and Iraqis already knew: nothing was being accomplished through this occupation, and it wasn't a secret. We all knew it, especially those with boots on the ground.

Still, our deployments continued. More boots were on the ground. More flag-draped caskets were transported home. More widows hung flags with one star in the middle of them, signifying their lost loved one. More children became war orphans. More field hospitals filled up with survivors of IED attacks.

Christmas Eve made me feel farther away from home than I had in six months of deployment. Something about it stung me. I was closer to where Jesus was born, but I felt further away from my faith and from myself than ever before. Violence reigned here, not light, and the feeling of hope I'd come to celebrate at Christmastime was absent. For the first time, I wasn't insulated from the pain that much of the world lives with year-round. I had a front-row seat to a place crying out for peace. Nothing felt right for any of us here. I ached to experience the hope breaking into darkness, the hope of Christmas in real life, not just reenactments on the darkened stage of a church.

"Medic!" The sergeant calling me shook me out of my dark thoughts as the Humvee pointed toward the safety of camp for the night. Our convoy of Humvees had stumbled into an accident scene on the road back to camp. A semitruck lay strewn across the sand as if a giant toddler had thrown a temper tantrum and hurled it down in his sandbox. The truck careened on its side at an impossible angle.

Luckily, it hadn't started on fire yet. If it had, the smoke and flames would have announced our presence for miles, and our hope for getting home safely after dark would have been even slimmer.

This stop was not in my plan. Word would travel through the local grapevine that a truck had overturned. The desert looked empty, but news traveled fast. Hunger and a lack of jobs made families desperate, and a truck filled with sellable goods could keep a family afloat for weeks. The crash would also alert the enemy to an easy opportunity to catch us in the open, stopped like sitting ducks. Stopping was risky, and we didn't have much time.

I grabbed my medic bag and threw it on my back as I ran toward the sound of "Medic!" being bellowed in the darkness. Two men lay in the sand, thrown from the truck as it jackknifed itself in the ditch. I couldn't believe they had survived the accident. These men weren't wearing my uniform. I didn't know whether they were my enemies or my allies. This war was so difficult because the enemy was always in camouflage—shooting while hiding behind a crowd of kids in a village, wearing civilian clothes, or in one of the many uniforms of other countries and suppliers. Staying alive required being suspicious of everyone, but as a medic, I served every single life on the battlefield with no discrimination. It wasn't my job to sort out who people were or weren't. A medic's code requires us to keep people alive and push back death, whether they are friend or foe.

I leaned down and listened for breath—a quick assessment, since I could hear one of them moaning in pain. Quickly, we loaded both of them into the back of the darkened Humvee, moving as fast as the unknown terrain would allow. And then the convoy was moving again, almost as quickly as it had stopped for the accident. Again we were passing through the darkened road, speeding toward safety and camp, slowly enough to navigate the torn-up road and quickly enough to make us think we were getting there.

Night had fallen now, the edges of dusk without a hint of light edging the eastern horizon. Ripping bandages, I worked in the semidarkness of the covered bed of the Humvee, praying my legs would keep me upright while the wheels bucked over the cratered road. I stabilized the spinal cord of one of my patients with a cervical spine collar, and thankfully, despite the darkness, I found an elusive vein to pump IV fluids into his body. This wasn't an ambulance, so the stretcher balanced across the crossbars close to the cab. The IV bag swung from the rib of the Humvee's soft roof covering. I kept working and swallowed down hard the anxiety I felt when this patient said he couldn't feel his legs. The other injured man sat on the wooden slats of one of the troop benches along the sides of the Humvee. We had only one stretcher, so he had to hold himself upright.

Coughing, he grabbed my attention from where he sat on the bench with the words I never wanted to hear from a patient. "I'm going to die. Tell my wife I love her," he wheezed, hand shaking as he struggled to hold the weight of the satellite phone he pushed into my hands. The hair on the back of my neck stood straight up, and I felt an icy-cold shock. Only one patient had ever uttered those words to me before; his heart stopped beating five minutes later in a hospital elevator, where he was being moved to the intensive-care unit to be monitored. I remember reassuring him, almost laughing, telling him, no, I wouldn't call his wife because his blood pressure was steady and his breathing was fine. He was fine. But death announces its coming arrival to a patient in a myriad ways, even if I couldn't see it myself.

My current patient was right. My medic brain put together the pieces as quickly as he had felt it. We were an hour away from camp, and one of his lungs had most likely collapsed from the impact of the accident. He wasn't going to make it to camp alive.

I needed to give him a hope I didn't have. Half the battle of keeping a patient alive is enlisting a patient's brain to help their body fight to stay alive. I needed him to believe he would live, to say it out loud like a battle cry. Because once the truth is on the table, it's like a shattered mirror, impossible to pick up and put back together. His words revealed a stark reality, and I needed to respond carefully.

My old us-versus-them mentality suddenly seemed simplistic and imaginary compared with the reality that was thumping in my chest. His life mattered, even though he wasn't an American soldier. If he died, something in me would die, too. I couldn't turn away from the reality of our connectedness and of God's love for us both, as equals. The truth was on the table sitting between us. It was undeniable.

As I stared into his eyes, I gently wrapped my hands around the satellite phone he was holding out to me, laying it down on the dusty green bench next to him. A jolt of unexpected confidence ignited my heart. "What's your name?" I asked him. "Xavier," he replied. And then words tumbled out of my mouth before I understood I was saying them. I heard myself saying, "I don't know what you believe, Xavier, but I believe in a God of life and not death. And tonight, on Christmas, we celebrate God breaking through the darkness and bringing life and hope to the whole world. So you tell your wife you love her yourself—because you're not dying tonight." Where this spontaneous eruption of faith and words came from, I don't know. But I was praying out loud, begging God to spare his life that night, asking God to push back death's creeping claim on his body.

Each breath he took ignited a glimmer of hope in us both. "Keep breathing, slow and steady," I murmured over and over as the Humvee took us closer to our camp's tent hospital. As one minute turned into ten minutes, his lungs kept struggling, but they weren't stopping. Every breath he took was an answer to my ragged prayer. He was bleeding from his head; the bandage I had wrapped around him was already soaked through. Blood traveled down his forehead, pushing his flickering eyelid closed. A bump in the road bounced his trembling shoulders forward, pushing him toward the floor. "Keep breathing," I whispered as I caught his shoulders and gently held his injured body back on the bench.

With each breath, something unexpected was taking place. I didn't know if he would live or not, but I knew what the biggest love I could imagine looked like: Xavier making it to camp alive. Life was breaking into the back of the dusty Humvee. Hope pulsed through me. The Humvee rolled to a stop. I heard voices outside before the medic on duty at the tent clinic opened the flap. My eyes squinted against the bright light streaming into the dark Humvee. We had arrived. Xavier wasn't dead.

The rocks crunched under my feet as I left the tent clinic. I mumbled to the medics, "Take care of him," but what I really meant to say was a confession—that he wasn't what we had been told to see him as: a "rag head," "enemy," or a "waste of our time." He was us, and we were him. The sparing of his life spared us all from different kinds of death.

The medics at the clinic didn't know that the patient they carried into the tent hospital carried a miracle in his breath. I had witnessed the hope of Christmas show up in the weariest part of the world. And I rejoiced.

* * *

Six months of war had changed how I saw God. I still believed God is love, but I just didn't understand why the Divine would allow human beings to do such ugly things to each other. Why wouldn't God intervene? When I enlisted, I believed I was doing what my God and my country wanted me to do. But now, the only thing I knew for sure was that God had asked me not to take a child's life to keep the convoy rolling. I couldn't escape this inner war that raged inside me.

I couldn't speak aloud my misgivings and pain at the violence I was part of. One morning, I found myself on the edge of my cot, and rather than standing up to head out to roll call for the day as usual, I clawed at my flak vest, ripping open the Velcro openings where one of the bulletproof plates slid into the vest to protect my chest from bullets and shrapnel. Reaching into the opening, my hands jerked out the bulletproof plate as if it had been burning my skin by being there, and I threw it on my cot. Relief flooded over me. I felt as if I could finally take a deep breath. A weight had been lifted off me. My shoulders felt freer. I pushed them back and stood up, taller now.

I realized that while I couldn't stop the violence around me, I could choose how I showed up in this war. I could choose how far I would go to protect my life at the expense of others. The bulletproof plates lying on the floor weren't my surrender; they were my fight song. Removing them was saying that the worst thing that could happen to me wasn't death. Choosing how I would show up in this unpredictable war felt right. I was just so sick and tired of death being used to scare me and tired of using death to scare someone else. I couldn't pick up my marbles and go home, but I could choose how I would fight.

I was fully responsible for my actions and how they affected another human being. Nothing could absolve me from that responsibility. My freedom wasn't free; my choices had consequences. I would choose love. Even if it cost me my life, I wouldn't really lose.

Six months into the war, nothing made sense to me. But removing these plates felt like coming up for air. I woke up like a caged bird every morning, fearing bombs, bullets, mangled battle buddies I wouldn't be able to save, or having to take life from someone else. Taking these plates out of my vest was me looking death in the face and saying, "You aren't the only thing that matters." Removing the bulletproof plates that made me safer wasn't a death wish or a reckless decision. It was me deciding what mattered most to me. My life wasn't the only valuable thing I had to lose. I was made by love, to love. That was the true identity I was beginning to find. I couldn't let fear and self-protection take that away from me.

The most powerful thing I'd ever experienced was a divine love. It was more than a loyalty to my country and to people who looked and talked like me. I was a soul who was connected to life, not just mine alone. Somehow Baby Muhammad's and Xavier's lives were entangled in mine, too. What watered my roots watered their roots. What hurt them hurt me. What gave me life put more life into the soil we all lived in. If one of our lives was taken, we all lost.

Standing up, my flak vest lighter now, I swung my medic bag onto my back and headed out the door, standing taller in my dusty combat boots than I had the day before. I felt more alive, more me. Fear of death didn't own me anymore. I pushed it back just enough to take a lifesaving breath. The war still pinned me against the wall, scaring the bejesus out of me, taunting me, but I had found my footing. My feet were standing on something solid, no longer on something shifting. I was more than my fear; I believed in something more beautiful than avoiding death. I wanted to learn how to truly live, not just survive. I didn't want to die, but I refused to keep living as if fear of death was my only master, so that everything I did, every choice I made, was justifiable because I did it in order to stay alive. I had better things to live my life for; avoiding death wasn't enough for me anymore.

7

Conscientious Objector

We know truth, not only by the reason, but also by the heart.
—Blaise Pascal, *Pensées* (1699)

It was the middle of the night when I woke up to my sergeant calling for a medic through the open tent flap. The call had traveled from the front of the tent like a slow-motion game of telephone, passed from sleepy soldier to sleepy soldier, until it reached my cot in the far corner. As if a bucket of ice water had been poured over my head, I woke up, instantly alert and ready to move. Nothing good results in calling for a medic in the middle of the night. Fumbling under my cot in the darkness, my hands caught the laces of my boots resting in their usual spot. I shook the boots upside down to clear out any desert snakes and spiders that liked to curl up for warmth inside them at night. My stomach churned for fear of what I was walking into. A whispered "This is not good" tumbled out of my mouth as I stood up.

My nine-millimeter Beretta was still warm from where it lay at night, sandwiched between my hip and the olive-colored cot—close at hand, just in case. I heaved my medic bag onto my back, and its worn straps found their familiar grooves between my shoulder blades as I stepped out into the starry darkness.

"Follow me," barked the night staff sergeant. He turned on a dime and strode toward our company's headquarters tent. As we walked, our boots crunched loudly on the newly laid gravel, spread to make a dry trail. During the rainy season, whole patches of desert turned into impassable, quicksand-like mud. "A slough," I thought to myself, remembering what my two farmer cousins in South Dakota called fields that had turned into expansive muddy lakes overnight. (As it happened, both of them would land with their National Guard unit at Balad Air Base north of Baghdad the same week I would fly home. All three of us would cross paths before I left the war.)

As I entered the command tent, my eyes blinked back at the glare of the light bulb overhead. A suffocating silence hung in the air, replacing the usual middle-of-the-night smoking and joking that was our unit's coping mechanism for bad hours, bad food, and bad situations.

The sergeant on duty sat behind a desk built with stray pieces of plywood. Head bent over a stack of papers, he didn't look up as he gave me my orders: "Take Sergeant Olson to the clinic to be stitched up and evaluated. Wait here for the paperwork."

Glancing up briefly, his eyes caught mine before he solemnly nodded toward a soldier sitting in a lone chair next to the tent's door. Sergeant Olson sat with his eyes fastened to the floor. I recognized him immediately. We had both attended drill weekends at the same armory across the street from my university campus. Despite knowing each other, we said nothing. The glaring white bandages wrapped around both his wrists told the story that no one dared to breathe out loud. Sergeant Olson must have believed, if only for a

On the day of the convoy, I saw these little girls running toward our truck as we drove past. I couldn't help wondering about the kids like them who might be pushed in front of a convoy on a different road, or on a different day.

My young friend from the village Awaijah and the crew of children that followed her everywhere.

At the end of the day, the desert sunsets were stunning to see.

Visiting one of my favorite families. One of the girls liked to take off my Kevlar helmet and try it on.

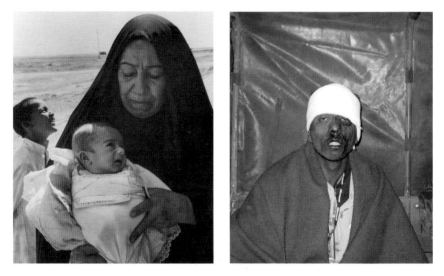

LEFT: Om Hassan, the woman who invited me into her home and trusted me before she knew if I was trustworthy. She changed my life with her act of preemptive love. She is carrying baby Mohammed after he came back from the hospital.

RIGHT: Xavier didn't die on Christmas Eve, he lived. His life is gritty, just like this photo. Surviving doesn't always look pretty, but it looks like holding on, even when it feels impossible. And Xavier did just that.

Spending time with the children in the village who escorted me everywhere.

In middle of the night, these people waited at the airport in Maine to welcome us home. My battle buddy (the one I shared an omelette with while our chow hall took a direct hit) and I had been waiting a year to finally touch our home soil again. We couldn't contain our excitement—we even threw on the sunglasses we found left on a bench in the airport.

ABOVE: My family: Jake, Bridger, and Zelalem. *Photo by Lyndsey Johnson*

LEFT: This was a special day for our family, when Zelalem received his citizenship at the courthouse.

LEFT: The march for Michael Brown was our family's first. Here's the sign Bridger wanted to get his picture taken with.

RIGHT: At the Orlando night club shooting vigil, Jake pinned a rainbow flag on each of our sons' chests after explaining what it meant.

Finally getting to meet the soapmakers whose story I'd been sharing with groups for years. Eating with Goze, Sozan, and their families was like getting to meet my real life heroes in person.

My teammate, Ihsan, and his beautiful family.

Erin relaxing with a business owner on one of our visits to a Syrian Refugee Camp.

LEFT: Spending time with Ihsan and his family is a dream come true.

BOTTOM LEFT: With Dr. Sabah Alwan at his house for dinner on Good Friday.

BOTTOM RIGHT: We celebrated Memorial Day with Veterans for Peace along the shore of Lake Superior in Duluth, MN. The sign says "Mourn the fallen, heal the wounded, work for peace."

Celebrating Valentines Day by raising money for Preemptive Love.

LEFT: The day Bridger and Zelalem went to their first day of Preschool.

RIGHT: We erased "pre" and took my first day of "school" photo. Jake bought me a school sweatshirt so I'd be legit at the college.

On the roof with the soapmaker's son at sunset.

few moments that evening, that suicide was the only way out of this war.

Although he continued to avoid my gaze, keeping his eyes fixed on his sand-encrusted boots, I forged through the suffocating silence like a snowplow in a Minnesota blizzard, snapped into medic mode, and attended to his bandaged wrists, lifting them gently from his lap. Turning them over, I retied knots and checked for pressure—strong radial pulses—while searching for the telltale sign of blood soaking through the layers, which would indicate the need for another pressure dressing.

I worked in silence, trying to preserve the military respect that Sergeant Olson deserved. Both of us knew his sergeant stripes would be stripped off, just as his bloody bandages would be. The Army wouldn't let this act of desperation go. No, they would deprive him of his rank and the authority to command troops. Living in a war zone is hard physically and psychologically. For soldiers who are forced to develop the mental, emotional, and physical toughness needed to survive, this kind of "weakness" cannot be tolerated within leadership ranks. Some war wounds are given ribbons and heavy medals; others are quietly punished by removing stripes and stripping people of their years of honorable service.

Armed with the correct paperwork, I walked a rebandaged Sergeant Olson across camp to the tent clinic, looking for a doctor to stitch him up.

While I waited on a dusty bench inside the clinic, the faded olive canvas slapping my back as the wind whipped, a soldier sitting next to me leaned over and interjected, "You're a medic, right? You must be a conscientious objector."

Conscientious objector? I didn't even know what that was, but the word *conscientious* immediately gripped me. It maneuvered between the seams of my empty flak vest, veering threateningly close to my heart. After months of subsisting on fear and constantly being fed an us-versus-them, "shoot first, ask questions later" mind-set, my head and heart were a minefield. I was a soldier in a war zone, but I still didn't know whether I could kill someone if I had to. I was hiding behind the medic bag I carried and the job that came with it—defending life, limb, or eyesight without exception. Wearing self-protective blinders, I zeroed in on keeping people alive long enough to get them transported and cared for. I accepted the possibility of having to watch people die, but I hadn't yet decided if I could pull the trigger to *take* a life.

Oblivious to my battling conscience, the soldier carried on this one-sided conversation. "Me too," he continued as if I had answered.

Refusing to meet his gaze, I kept my eyes on the floor, staying in my protect-and-defend mode, which I had practiced so well as a lone female soldier: *Don't look up. Be small, invisible, less female, less me. Avoid being noticed. And try to make it through another day without being pinned against a wall or targeted for following to the latrine at night.*

That didn't deter him from continuing to talk. "I'm not an *official* conscientious objector," he clarified in a cheerful voice. "But I love Jesus, and there's no way I would take away another person's chance at knowing God's love by taking their life." His words sounded like an official pronouncement, cutting through the silence of the deserted clinic waiting area. "I'm a truck driver, and it's dangerous out there every day. And I love my wife and two kids back home. But I refuse to load bullets in my weapon," he declared. "I'd rather go to heaven myself than take that opportunity away from another person."

I was stunned. His words were like a neon sign illuminating a truth that had been chasing me since landing in this war: *What am I willing to give my life for? What am I willing to take a life for?*

My unflinching answer to both those questions had always been America. I had always been satisfied by this answer until the first night of the convoy. My certainty trembled under the weight of this soldier's commitment to a costly, self-sacrificing love. God's quiet insistence that he loves my enemy too pushed back on my beliefs that night.

The soldier beside me was the first person I'd met who thought this way. I caught a glimmer of a love so big that death couldn't scare it into doing anything other than loving the other person. His faith made him free in a way I wasn't. He was free to live as if heaven was real and this earth was not his home, and he could live out that faith in the most costly way imaginable—as if he had something extravagant to give, instead of something priceless to protect.

Sitting on the bench in the tent clinic, I felt a hovering elation. The truest and most beautiful love I could imagine was sitting right next to me, smiling to himself. His cross-shaped love started to unmake the fear that had been suffocating my soul on the battlefield. The tension that had been building ever since the night God told me not run over an Iraqi child to protect my convoy finally broke.

I understood that I could follow God's command to love my enemy *and* serve the country I love. But what had felt like holding in tension two competing allegiances—my allegiance to my country and my allegiance to God—was actually an unequal match. One allegiance trumped the other.

I understood that my faith does not require me to kill as proof of my loyalty. It requires me to give myself away, to love my enemies instead of hating them.

I understood that I couldn't be whole if I took the life of another.

But if I gave my life in sacrificial love for someone else, then I wouldn't really lose.

I understood that no matter what flag we were born under or what uniform we wear, we are all in the same family, the human family—planted in the same soil, roots intertwined.

I understood that I no longer had to choose between my own life and someone else's. I could choose both. Because there is absolutely something more precious to lose than your own life.

I understood that my faith is a call to come fully alive, not just dodge death.

With that understanding, the burden I'd been carrying since stepping onto the battlefield lifted from my shoulders like a hot-air balloon suddenly freed from the gravity that had been pinning it to the ground. Untethered, I could see what I had been blind to my whole life—that I was made for life, not death, that even if I gave my life away, I could never really lose. Sometimes we have to be willing to die in order to come fully alive.

So in the middle of the night, in a dusty tent in Iraq, I looked the truck-driving soldier in the eye and said, "Me too."

* * *

Later that night back in my tent, sitting on the edge of the army cot that represented my three feet of living space among twelve other soldiers, I held my nine-millimeter Beretta in my hands. It suddenly felt heavy, almost too heavy to hold.

I slid my thumb along the side until it found the magazine release. I heard a metallic *click,* and a full magazine tumbled out into my hands. The gold glint of fifteen bullets shone brightly in my palm. Holding it in my trembling left hand, I reached under my cot with my right hand and pulled out my metal ammo case. A camel sticker with the

Kuwaiti flag waved up at me. I lifted the case onto my lap, unclasped the lid, and flung it open, flipping the smiling-camel sticker decor upside down. My left hand hovered over the open ammo box, where my second magazine was stored as usual for the night.

That soldier's words were still ringing in my ears, still pounding in my chest. Adrenaline pumped through me, leaving a strange metallic aftertaste in my mouth. I wouldn't recognize him if I passed him in the chow hall the next day, but the words he had spoken were electrifying. They were breaking open a new possibility, a third way I had never heard of before.

Clink. My thumb flicked the first bullet out of the magazine. It landed in the bottom of the box with a loud metal *clunk*. My thumb found the ridge of the next bullet and released it from the magazine's spring. It tumbled down into the ammo box after the first bullet. The spring of the magazine tore into my thumb. With each bullet I released, its pressure lessened. The thrum in my chest quieted in sync with the bullets being ejected. As the last round left the magazine, I heard its telltale click of spring against spring, instead of bullet against bullet.

Now empty, the magazine felt like a feather resting on my upturned palm. I pushed it back into its place, inside the pistol grip of my Beretta. My weapon didn't look any different than before. No one would be able to tell it didn't hold its standard-issue fifteen rounds. But nothing would ever be the same for me again.

My head sunk onto my chest. Grateful tears streamed down my cheeks. My shoulders slumped in relief, as if they'd had been holding up the pyramids and were just relieved of the crushing weight.

Peace flooded over me, down my face, into my chest, allowing me to take deep, refreshing breaths of cool air. Freed from taking a life, I felt closer to God than I had since I'd stepped into this war zone.

It was the comforting presence of true freedom and the absence of a false sense of security.

The next day, for the first time since landing in Iraq, I woke up without fear clawing in my belly. I finally knew who I was. I am a citizen of heaven first and a patriot second. God's call to love my enemy would take first place. I was set free. There was so much peace in knowing I would step in front of a bullet for anyone but wouldn't use a bullet to take a life.

I was still scared of the possibility of watching one of my soldiers get blown up in front of me and not being able to save their life. I was still scared of being raped by my fellow soldiers or tortured by the enemy. But the freedom of knowing *how* I was going to face those fears in the midst of war changed everything.

It brought me back to what I'd known all along: that love is the most powerful weapon on the planet. At church, I had learned that love can transform enemies into friends, fear into friendship, even hate into humility. When the world was broken, God gave—not conquered—to heal it. God sacrificed to make things whole again. My tradition puts the cross everywhere to make clear that self-sacrifice is the way to make wrongs right. And it is *that* kind of selfless, transformative, fearless love that I am called to give away. This was my only debt: to love the way I was loved.

Seeing myself first and foremost as an outpost of love, a citizen of heaven, changed the way I saw the war, my enemies, and the world around me—it rearranged everything. Believing that this earth is not my home—and living that out—made me feel free. I was alive to living life without doling out death, and nothing could take that away from me. The fear of death no longer controlled me. The pressure to be willing to kill to prove my allegiance to the country

I love was lifted. It couldn't make me rain down death when I was created to rain down life and more life on this earth.

Even in the midst of unpredictable violence, hope bubbled up in me. As with a foot that has fallen asleep, the waking was painful and exhilarating. I was coming alive, in a place where I had been slowly dying.

* * *

The missions kept coming, and days rolled into months as we loaded up the trucks in the early-morning darkness and drove back home through the checkpoint when the sun was starting to set. Alpha Company moved from our tent city halfway up to Baghdad to replace a unit that was redeploying home. I was given orders to be attached to them for the mission. The task was to go up and down a main highway and sweep it for IEDs, ambushes, and snipers.

After we finished our first clean sweep of the highway on our mission, the brand-new second lieutenant signaled for us to leave the main road and drive down a small dirt road. His bright-brown uniform with its crisp creases stood out amidst our faded brown camouflage uniforms, dusty and worn from six months in the desert. He had just finished Officer Candidate School and shipped out to become our new second lieutenant a week ago.

The farther we drove down the road, the more uneasy I started to feel. Big trucks need wide roads to turn around—or to run away from an ambush. This road was starting to feel suffocating. "This road isn't looking good, Lieutenant," the driver of the Humvee shouted over the rumbling engine. I repositioned my medic bag at my feet nervously, while stealing a glance at the face of the other soldier in the back of the Humvee with me. His eyes nervously darted back at me, and he held his weapon uncharacteristically at the ready. The air was heavy with something none of us liked.

Before the lieutenant responded to the driver's warning to turn around, shots rang out. Yelling erupted inside the Humvee. "Get us out of here now!" the lieutenant barked, hand slapping down on the metal dashboard. The metallic bursts of gunshots exploded in the air around us.

After our convoy was out of the range of fire and back safely onto the main road, our adrenaline popped like a champagne cork, and everyone started talking on top of each other. "I can't believe we were just shot at!" "It came out of nowhere!" "Now that we've been shot at, we earned our combat patches." I looked away, eyes locked on the horizon. Cold relief rolled down my back while the pounding in my chest slowed down. We were safe—at least for the time being.

Not wearing my bulletproof plates in my flak vest or loading bullets in my weapon didn't make me more or less afraid, even after taking fire. Every day, I felt like I was balancing a rock of fear and worry on my chest, and unloading my weapon didn't change that. But what my choice did do was give me a way to push back against something I had grown to hate: death, along with the way people felt justified in doing anything to another person if their own life was threatened.

I was tired of being afraid of someone killing me, and I was tired of the way my uniform seemed to strike fear in those around me. I wanted to punch death in the face and take away some of its power over me. Death couldn't scare me into being someone I wasn't. Taking out my bulletproof plates felt like taking back some of my humanity. It felt like reclaiming a truth, claiming light in the middle of a stretch so dark I couldn't see through it to what the end looked like.

Disarming in the middle of a war did make me less safe. I felt the weight of that choice every day of my deployment. In an unpredictable war, I couldn't choose what would happen to me, but I could choose how I showed up in it. No bullets, no plates—these were my terms.

When Torture Has a Face

Do not just slay your demons; dissect them and find what they've been feeding on.
—Andres Fernandez, *Simple Twist of Fate: The Man Frozen in Time*

Grabbing my hands, Fatima tugged me along, forcing me to run up the village path to keep pace with her. Something was buzzing in the air in Awaijah, and it had drawn me toward the tumble of houses squatting on the hill-lined path. Like a red sky in the morning alerting sailors to bad weather, the children who were often running and playing in groups outside their homes alerted me to the happenings of the village. Fatima, the leader of the kids, who escorted me to each house when I arrived at the village, locked her hand around my wrist, swatting away the boys' hands that reached for mine.

She was an overbearing traffic cop, directing the other children with a sharp glare and forceful hand motions, although for me, she had only smiles and shy hugs. In contrast to a traffic cop's crisp uniformed hat, she had hair that reached for the sky in every direction. In her eye was a Peter Pan look of adventure, and she carried herself with confidence that made you follow her into the next house or up around the bend. Her enthusiasm never dampened, even though the adults in every house we entered clucked and scolded as they attempted to push down her wild hair with slathers of spit.

Today, as I was carried up the hill in the middle of a current of village children, the buzz of excitement was palpable. My five-foot frame blended into the throng, despite the nine-millimeter Beretta strapped to my hip and the flak vest hanging with medic scissors, airway openers for trauma, tape, tourniquets, ammo pouches, and Kevlar helmet with nighttime glow in the dark cat eyes. None of this gear repelled my young friends from touching me. They saw past this part of me and took me in with a sureness that made me shy. They believed in a good in the world, and even though my uniform represented the violence that shaped their daily life, they wouldn't allow it to stop them from taking my hand and living as if Neverland were real.

I wondered if something had happened to Baby Muhammad. He had been doing so well lately. Since his triumphant homecoming from the camp hospital, Baby Muhammad's story had traveled back to my home, launching a flow of packages of formula in return. I had been delivering a can of baby formula for him every week or two. Over time, his cheeks bloomed and became so chubby that they filled up your hands when you rocked him. His eyes sparkled as his body sprouted. He was still the prize of the village, and he often wound up in my arms the minute I sat down. The clucks and smiles of all of his aunties landed on him, and I joined in. We'd sigh and breathe in his dark eyes and the magic of his contented coos. Something about his little life echoed hope into the dusty routine of our days. But as it turned out, Fatima wasn't bringing me to see Baby Muhammad.

At the home of Om Hassan, the matriarch of Awaijah, the children pushed me through the door, and I ducked out of the blazing sunlight into the calm shadows. As my eyes adjusted to the semidarkness, I saw that the house was packed with people. There was hardly room to stand. Taking off as much of my battle rattle as I could, I leaned against the wall. Bringing a weapon and even wearing combat boots in a family's home gnawed at me. It felt disrespectful and oppressive, not to mention conspicuous. But Om Hassan's friendship reached past my outward appearance. The goodness and generosity of her choice to embrace me still made me blush. I couldn't shed the reality that I was part of the army that had invaded her country and ruled it with force. For better or worse, this was who I was. This is where I was.

Barreling toward me, Om Hassan grabbed my hands and launched into a tornado of Arabic. We usually went achingly slow and used a lot of touching and hand motions to communicate, but today she left me behind in the stampede of words. Seeing my blank face, she realized I hadn't caught on to why there was so much celebrating in the room. She darted into the crowded living room and came back with an elderly man and the biggest smile I'd ever seen on her face. The room's buzz quieted down as he stood in front of me.

Slowly and deliberately, she announced in shy English, "Diana, this is my husband."

None of this made sense. Om Hassan was the leader of the village because her husband had been taken during the Iran-Iraq War. When she had told me her husband wasn't dead, but a POW, I thought it was a cultural norm or just a wildly hopeful family story. For almost a year, I had been part of this family's village life, and now

I was standing in front of the patriarch of the whole village. This was why the village was buzzing. He was home!

His eyes sparkled as he looked at me shyly. She hurriedly put my hands where his ears should have been. "You," she motioned to me with her short arms expansively, "help him! They cut off his ears." I flinched as she pushed my hands deeper into the scar tissue ridges where his ears had been cut off of. My fingers flinched as I realized that I was touching a man who had been tortured, cut, and brutalized. "You help him," she repeated as she beamed and pointed to the medic bag on my back. She expected me to try to do what I'd always done—reach into my medic bag and make any ailment of a villager a little less bad. But this was different.

Moving my hands down from his ears, she placed them near his mouth and gestured toward his mouth. He attempted to talk, but only guttural sounds tumbled out. I couldn't understand him. Quizzically, I looked from her to him. Was I misunderstanding him because of my limited Arabic skills? Without embarrassment or missing a beat, he caught my confusion and mimed sticking out his tongue, and his other hand swooshed down, slicing the air like a knife. His tongue had been cut out. The realization made my stomach lurch. I pushed down the nausea and pushed a smile back into my face. His twinkling eyes stayed locked on mine. Begging myself to have the courage and military bearing to stay with him in the moment instead of crumble and to stay with Om Hassan in her long-awaited moment of celebration.

The room was celebrating his return, singing with joy and abandon. I couldn't let my revulsion at what human beings will do to each other in war dampen the joy in his family. They had held out hope for over a decade, believing he was alive. Today, they rejoiced over him and hugged each other. His adult children were finally able to embrace their papa again and introduce him to their husbands and children. I would allow myself to cry in my cot later that night but not now. I wouldn't think about how useless my medic bag would be to help his hearing or his pain. Om Hassan beamed at me, and I squeezed her hand back tight. We passed a smile back and forth between us—the same sort of smile that we shared at the tent hospital after hearing the news that Baby Muhammad would live.

She had held her family together as tightly as she could, trying to shield them against the violence that camped out by her village. Watching her, I witnessed the fierceness of her love unfolding like an umbrella, covering all the daughters, sons, and grandchildren.

I can imagine her as a young woman, with wind-tossed hair, steely resolve in her eyes, leading her people through the next impossibility. War didn't rob her of her humanity; it sharpened it. It didn't scare her into guarding her life; it propelled her into living it out to the fullest. She looked at death in all its forms as it nipped at her family's heels—scarce food, dirty water, checkpoints and armed soldiers, sickness—and defiantly said, "Watch me live." She fought with love instead of hate. She chose to trust someone she was told was her enemy. She was the bravest warrior on this battlefield, because she fought for all of us—not just her people, not just her side.

* * *

That night, lying on my cot in the darkness, I finally allowed the tears to find their way down my cheeks and onto my pillow. This was my first war, but it wasn't theirs. My fingers still felt burning heat from where they had touched the remnants of Om Hassan's husband's ears—my hands, on either side of his smiling face, his eyes dark brown with flashes of green planted into the tops of his irises. The memory of looking into his eyes, feeling the parts of his body mutilated from torture tore at the seams of my world, was ripping part of me in half. How could human beings do this to another human being?

I had believed in torture in the same way that I grew up passively accepting that killing was a necessary evil to protect and defend my country. I hadn't ever spent much time thinking about whether I would kill or not, but I accepted that other people did it for my benefit, for my security. I had separated myself from the spiritual weight of what I allowed someone to do on my behalf. And I had maintained that same level of distance during basic training when I trained to survive as a POW. State my name, my rank, and the Geneva Convention code that prohibits torture and inhumane treatment of POWs. Refuse to tell any information about my unit, our location, or our missions. Wait to be freed.

I had accepted the idea of torture—that it is a necessary evil used in war to protect innocent lives. But that was before I put my hands on the ears and looked into the eyes of a human being who had been cut with knives. And that was before I learned that my fellow soldiers had been caught torturing Iraqi prisoners in Abu Ghraib prison, two hours north of me—not because they had been told to, not because they had been ordered to extract confessions or information. Their prisoners hadn't been convicted of a crime. The soldiers chose to torture them.

Face-to-face with a person who had been tortured, all I could see in his face was my grandpa's sun-wrinkled smile and twinkling eyes. The way my grandpa's leathery face lit up when he was surrounded by his family was just like Om Hassan's husband's face when he was surrounded by his family. How long had he held out before his captors decided he didn't know any more and they could cut out his tongue without sacrificing vital information? How did he not bleed to death or succumb to fevers from infection?

If my grandpa had been tortured while he was in the military, it would be wrong. The torture of Om Hassan's husband also was wrong. On the night after I met Om Hassan's husband, I asked myself how I had accepted the idea of torture without seeing the reality of the other human being on the receiving end. The answer made my stomach sink and my shoulders slump forward. I had put myself first and erased the way violence landed on other people. My security, my country—the rest of the story didn't matter. My narrative ended with me. I felt complicit for never having questioned the validity of torture as long as it was for my security and as long as it was my country who did the torturing. Torturing a human being is wrong, no matter who does it.

Finding myself connected to Om Hassan, Baby Muhammad, and Xavier showed me my place in the worldwide family of seven billion people. My beliefs and the impact they have on others didn't feel too large or far away; they were zoomed in like a microscope on how my actions were connected to more than just me. It forced me to pull my truths out of my pocket, unfold them, and lay them down on the family table and ask hard questions. If an action harms another person, it can't really be good for me, because our roots are wrapped around one another. I claim to follow a two-thousand-year-old tradition that defines itself with the symbol of a cross—a dying to self for the resurrecting of love, to love my neighbor as well as I love myself, to join God in the dying and resurrecting of other-love instead of self-love. All my beliefs in "necessary evils" suddenly sounded hollow, like cheap excuses to put myself first.

Coming face-to-face with Om Hassan and her husband's tortured body ripped off my blinders. I could see clearly that the Iranian soldiers who had tortured him weren't any different from my fellow American soldiers who used torture. Each soldier believed and was told the same thing: that it was their duty and their right to put their interests first. But I was coming alive to the reality that the human family is bigger than any one country can hold, and the Creator who made every person on the planet doesn't play favorites the same way I did.

War isn't holy; it's our human tradition. It comes from wanting what we don't have and using violence to get it. You can't bring peace on earth when you use weapons of war. You can't build up God's kingdom of love, mercy, forgiveness, and self-sacrifice using the tools of death, deception, and destruction.

Jesus interrupted violence; he didn't use it. We can choose to live like Christ. But we can't take a life like Christ, because he never did. So war is counter to the ways of Jesus, because war uses tools Jesus wouldn't touch to mend the broken things of the world. Human history says that we can't live without war, that we need it, while Jesus tells us we won't truly live until we can give it up. I don't know what it means to love my enemies, but refusing to kill or to accept torture is a first step.

* * *

The day after I met Om Hassan's husband, my company was tasked with a new mission. We were to pack up and move to Camp Scania, an outpost halfway to Baghdad, to clear the main highway of bombs and IEDs each day. If we found and disarmed the devices before they were detonated by a family in a car driving to school or a soldier in a Humvee on their mission for the day, we could save lives and keep the main supply route open. Supply routes are the arteries in war, supplying food, water, bullets, and gasoline to keep the fighting force fighting.

Up until the day I left Iraq, I was still waiting to see my friends in a Awaijah again. Out on missions, I'd ask Iraqis I met on the side of the road about the village and asked if they could pass messages to them. Off and on, I'd bump into a soldier or Iraqi who told me my friends said hello from the village. There wasn't much functioning electricity, internet, or phone service, but communication happened. People were always moving from one place to another, bringing news and relaying messages.

I never saw Om Hassan again. I never got to help her husband's ears or find out more of his story. I didn't know that the day on which I felt her squeeze my hand as she celebrated the return of her husband would be our last meeting. If I had known that it was to be the last time I would see her, I would have told her this: you taught me how to live, and it has changed me forever.

9

Homecoming

That this is your country, that this is your world, that this is your body. And you must find some way to live within the all of it.
—Ta-Nehisi Coates, *Between the World and Me*

The ground attack alarm blared like a deafening tornado warning, so loud I couldn't hear anything else. I knew it was telling me to hurry up and do something, but I didn't know what. People started running in every direction, as if they were on fire. I knew soldiers don't run unless they've been ordered to. Panicking, I grabbed at one of the soldiers running past me in the dark and shouted, "Where are you going?"

"It's a ground attack," he yelled as he rushed past me, barely slowing down. "Find an underground bunker, and wait for the all-clear signal." Seeing my blank look, he looked over his shoulder and grabbed my arm between strides, ordering, "Follow me!"

My heart pounded as I felt the near miss of being left aboveground during an attack. I followed him through the throngs of chaos and when he turned left and suddenly stepped down through a trapdoor into an underground bunker. There was no sign, no marker; I don't know how he knew where it was in the dark. My battle buddy and I stumbled into his back as he slowed to go inside. The bunker was pitch-black but had the warm, sticky feeling of a rush-hour subway car packed with bodies. The smell of dirt and dampness surrounded us in the darkness.

"First time?" someone asked me from out of the blackness. Stumbling into the bunker had broadcast my newbie status or that Balad wasn't my home base camp.

"Yeah," I mumbled into the dark.

The siren and the sound of people running above us made me rethink what I had considered my good fortune to have left Camp Scania to be at Camp Balad, waiting for an airplane to go home. That unexpected move had occurred just three days previously. Our battalion of 500 soldiers had received orders to decamp and move up to Balad Air Base to wait for transport planes to finally take us home. We had been in Iraq for 397 days.

Balad was the answer to my prayer, but in the bunker, I started to get an uneasy feeling in my stomach. What if this was one of those flukes? I survive a whole year in war, and the week I'm waiting to get on the plane home, I'm caught in a ground attack. This was the second near miss in one night. Earlier that night, I had met up with two of my cousins from South Dakota, who had just landed in country for their deployment. We met up at Balad's functioning movie theater. Balad, which during Saddam's presidency was an Olympic training camp, had amenities I didn't believe existed during wartime. My cousins and I had just had a mini family reunion, eating whole pizzas in our seats and watching the only movie playing, *Hidalgo*—two hours of Viggo Mortensen racing his pony through the dry, hot, lonely, dusty desert. It had been so long since I had eaten pizza or sat in a movie theater that I didn't even mind that the movie was based in a desert, mirroring the scenery I was hoping to leave behind when we got on the plane. As we were walking out of the movie theater, a boom cracked through the quiet. Fire lit up the night, racing up the far side of the building. A rocket-propelled grenade (RPG) had hit the building. The attack came out of nowhere, its light burning my retinas against the night sky. Looking up at each other, my cousins, yelled over the siren, "Good luck!" as they ran to their battalion to check in. I turned and took off in the opposite direction toward my battalion's headquarters.

Walking out of a movie theater minutes before it gets bombed had felt eerie. Sitting in an underground bunker with a second ground attack going on overhead an hour later started to feel a little ill fated. I realized that getting on those planes home was going to be harder than I had thought.

* * *

The next day, my battle buddy and I walked past the closest chow hall, because we were going to partake in another indulgence at Camp Balad: made-to-order omelettes. We didn't mind the line; we had made it through a year of war and bad food. We had a transport flight home with Alpha Company's name on it. We had won the lottery on all counts and were going to soak up our good luck by standing in line for the best omelette of the year. Like friends waiting in line for a concert, we kept smirking at each other, as if to say, "How lucky are we?" Then, with our omelettes in to-go boxes cradled in our arms like trophies, we looked around the room for open seats. The whole first dining room was full, without a single place to sit. We walked into the second and looked around; in every direction, tan and brown shoulders were packed around tables just as full as the first. Pushing on the exit doors, we left the chow hall and climbed to the top of a neighboring hill, where we sat cross-legged and opened our still-steaming prize omelettes.

After we took our first bite, a whistle sang over our heads as an incoming rocket tore through the morning stillness. The back end of the chow hall we had just exited took a direct hit. Smoke billowed above the building, rising into the sparkling blue sky. As we looked down from our perch, not 500 feet away, flames licked the sides of the building, and black smoke poured into the morning air. Scrambling to our feet, we looked first at each other and then at the burning chow hall we had just walked out of. We didn't have to say it, but we both knew that if we had arrived five minutes later or had found somewhere to sit inside, we would have been in the chow hall when it was bombed instead of safely on the hill.

We left our omelettes on the ground on the hilltop. The ambulance sirens joined the camp's incoming warning signal. As we walked down the hill, we avoided watching the stretchers carrying the wounded out of the building. Home felt farther away than ever. Leaving Iraq would not be easy, I realized, if I even made it out alive.

* * *

After four uneasy days, we flew from Balad to Bangor, Maine, where I would first touch down on American soil. Walking off the tarmac, I was so excited I thought I would burst. After a thirteen-hour transatlantic flight inside a plane that turned meat locker cold when it reached its cruising altitude with minimal heat, I was chilled to the bone. All that kept me warm was the flicker of hope I held that I was finally going home.

When we landed, I walked into a darkened regional airport in the middle of the night. Tears began streaming down my face when I saw a solitary senior citizen who had come out in the middle of the night to welcome us home. She wasn't our loved ones, but she had chosen to be their replacement until we saw them in person. She extended her hand and said, "Welcome home." Overcome with a tidal wave of feeling, I launched myself into her arms for a hug and squeezed her fragile shoulders a little too hard. She wasn't my family, but in that moment, she felt like it. The next plane would leave me where I had started: Fort McCoy, Wisconsin.

Seven days later, after 397 days of living in a war, I found myself bewildered, driving the wrong way on the freeway. Duluth's freeway is like a marble run, simple with a few places to drop off the main drag. But somehow I had missed my turn. One week at Fort McCoy wasn't long enough to convince my head and my body that I wasn't in war anymore. Changing my habits back into peacetime living should have been automatic. But it wasn't. My only possessions were a bath towel and a pair of tennis shoes; everything else had been put in storage a year earlier or given back to the Army. I was floating on the wind, unable to get a firm grip on the place that used to be familiar. I wasn't familiar anymore.

Homecoming tested my survival skills in a way that leaving for war hadn't. Going into the unknown, you expect it to be unfamiliar. Coming home, you expect it to be familiar, so when it wasn't, that was terrifying. It was lonely. It felt like hovering above myself, unable to make my feet touch solid ground. When my company and I were deployed, we were thrown into a wartime world, with different rules for a different world. Back home, everyone else had simply lived another year of their regular life. When I finally reunited with my friends and family, words seized up in my throat, unable to bridge the gap between their "normal" year and my experience in war. I felt like their world had kept turning but mine had not—as if I'd spent a year living on the moon, a place they had never been and I couldn't describe. I couldn't speak their language, and they couldn't seem to speak mine.

Survival instincts took over. Without consciously deciding to, I wore the mask of the person I used to be, the way I wore my flak vest in Iraq, to reassure the people I loved that I was OK and to blend in. The Army hadn't known I took the bulletproof plates out of my flak vest, and back home my friends didn't know I was a peacemaker. When I was alone, I was bewildered. I had no idea who I was or if I had permission to be me. All I knew was that the person I had been didn't exist anymore. The Diana who had left for war didn't come back.

* * *

For most of the people I knew or encountered, the Iraq experience met them on the couch at night while CNN gave thirty seconds of war updates between the nightly news and their shows. But I had lived my Iraq experience twenty-four hours a day with the taste of fear and the feel of gritty sand in my mouth. I was part of the first wave of those who went to war as the preemptive strike, and I was in the first wave of soldiers to return.

When I returned to my job on the hospice/oncology ward at Saint Luke's Hospital, my service in Iraq started a lot of conversations. They usually went like this: A patient would ask, "What's that military ribbon on your uniform?" I would reply, "It's my combat ribbon. I just got back from serving as a combat medic in Iraq for a year." Then he—it was almost always a he—would take the conversation by the wheel and drive it for the next ten or fifteen minutes, telling me what was happening and what we really needed to do to "beat those bastards." Moving the blood pressure cuff above

94

his elbow, I'd nod and pump up the cuff, gathering my readings as he informed me about the situation in Iraq. Pulse taken, I'd reach above him to readjust his IV drip and double-check that the right antibiotic was flowing. All the while, he'd be spouting his opinions about the war I'd been fighting in and what he thought about "those people there." I would ask him to breathe in through his mouth, setting my stethoscope on the right side of his back to hear his lungs clearly. By the time I had repositioned him and given his meds for the day, I was ready to retreat from the onslaught of memories his flippant remarks and unquestioned authority dragged to the surface. Conversations like this made me feel invisible—as though my experience was erased in light of his opinions. And this happened in room after room with patient after patient. If a patient ever did make room for me in the conversation, it was to fire this question at me: "Did you kill anybody over there? See any action?"

If I had just gotten back from Disneyland three months ago, patients would have asked me how it was. But since I had just returned from war, they *told* me how it was. Why wouldn't they accept an eyewitness account as more valid than their television-informed opinion? I wondered if they would ask me my opinion of war if I were a burly male with the classic Army tattoo on my arm. The experience of being used, discounted, and dismissed for a man's benefit had quietly followed me back across the ocean to my home. Though I had changed my uniform from my desert camo fatigues to my ice-blue nursing scrubs, what was required of me hadn't changed. I was still expected to be small, to deny my own experience and accomplishments so the man in front of me could have an audience.

After a month of being forced to listen to insights into how "'the war in Iraq really is," I had had enough. It was too painful for me. Everything about it hurt my insides until I ached all over and didn't know how to make it stop. After my shift, I looked into the mirror and caught a glimmer of the culprit: the one-inch combat ribbon pinned over my heart on the left side of my nursing uniform. The ribbon went along with my Army Commendation Medal, Army Achievement Medal, and a coin I'd received from the commander of the whole southern region of operations in Iraq, the colonel of the 264th Engineer Brigade.

The day I received that medal in Iraq, my head was pounding, and I was curled up on my cot, dehydrated and sick, while we were stationed in a tiny patch of dirt called Camp Scania during the last three months of my deployment. The sergeant came in and said, "The colonel is smoking the whole company," which meant he was putting everyone in formation and putting them through push-ups and running drills until no one could do it anymore. Colonels typically pushed physical training before handing out awards, so my sergeant urged me, "Get your sick self out there now. They are asking for you."

I stood at attention in front of the colonel who commanded the southern war operations—from south of Baghdad to the coast at Basra—my hands tight at my sides, thumbs lined up along the seams of my pant legs, back ramrod straight, feet locked in, shoulders back in a straight line, holding down the queasiness of standing up for the first time that day. "You're a medic, soldier?"

"Yes, sir," I belted out through a sore throat and pounding headache.

"You any good at it?" he barked loudly, so everyone could hear him.

"Yes, sir!" I pushed the bald truth out into the desert air.

"Well, I hear you are the best damn medic in the whole 724th

Engineer Battalion. Soldier, accept this coin because of your service to your company, your battalion, and the United States of America."

I was proud of my service that day, and I still am today. But after my return home and my experiences with patients talking at me, I found myself pulling the pin off my chest, loosening the small clasps, and laying the ribbon on the counter as my shoulders heaved with relief. There would be no more dismissiveness from patients, no more lectures about my war. I was done being used for other people to hear the sound of their own voice. I didn't know how to have a voice or stand up for myself; my soul was too battered from the using and abusing and preying upon me that I'd experienced in the war. But I did know how to zip up the real me and make her smaller to survive. So I took off the ribbon. Closing the drawer, I knew I wouldn't let the ribbon see the light again anytime soon. It had just become another casualty.

★ ★ ★

My dad had bought me my service ribbon. When he gave it to me, he said, "Here, you should wear it on your nursing uniform. You should be proud of your service." I wasn't sure whether my dad was proud of his own service or why was it so important to him that I displayed mine. During the Vietnam War, he had been sleeping on the beach in New Jersey, with no money, hoping to go to acting school, when his draft number became so inevitable that it propelled him to enlist so he could pick his job: air traffic controller. I know he feels lucky that he wound up serving not in Vietnam, but in a tiny air field in Germany, where he met my mother.

While I didn't know whether he was proud of his service, I knew that I wanted to keep my wounds and my memories hidden—to avoid the often reflexive "Thank you for your service" from strangers.

I didn't want to be thanked. I wanted to be able to breathe in my own skin instead of being used by someone else to hear their own opinions or agree with them.

My new front line was coming home from war as a third-generation Army veteran but believing in something unfamiliar: peace and a faith that values my enemy as much as myself. Coming home from war as a peacemaker created a battlefield I wasn't prepared for. Instead of being the medic, I was the walking wounded. I was limping in ways I couldn't understand. PTSD named part of it, but I had no words to name the other wounds I was experiencing.

The military was all I knew. I come from a family and a church that have embraced only one way to honor and serve our country. If others didn't believe the way we did, baptize the way we did, or mirror our patriotism, we discounted them as not being true Americans or true Christians. I knew if I shared my battlefield experience of taking the bullets out of my weapon and my story of God asking me not to take a life, I would become "other" to the people I loved most. I would lose being part of the "us" in my family. I knew this, because it's what I thought before I went to war.

The hardest part about coming home a peacemaker was knowing I didn't belong. It was dangerous not to belong in war, in my unit as a female soldier, but it was deadly to my soul to realize I no longer belonged at home either. I didn't know how to explain that all soldiers believe in peace, that it's why we are willing to go to war. No one goes to war expecting more war. We believe peace is possible and it's worth fighting for.

I didn't feel like I had freedom to support the troops *and* refuse to support this war. Even the combat patch I earned didn't feel like it bought me the freedom to speak the truth out loud without being branded disloyal to my family, my faith, and my country. Freedom wasn't free, and I knew it. So I stayed quiet about my experience in Iraq. I traded my battlefield truth for belonging.

I thought surviving war would be the hard part. I thought I was home free the minute the plane touched down in America. I was wrong. The most painful days were ahead of me.

10

Raising Peacemakers

If at my funeral my enemies can say the same things about me as my friends,
I'll know I lived as a peacemaker.
—Erin Wilson, senior field editor, Preemptive Love, Iraq

I just couldn't face it. Thinking about the loud music and the bustle of people made my heart beat fast and my mouth go dry. I was waiting outside my church, trying to make myself walk through the door for the first time since coming back from war. Nothing about it felt familiar. In war, we avoided grouping together, because it made you an easy target for an attack, so entering a crowded church felt terrifying.

My friend Lauri saw me frozen in place. "Wanna go in and see everyone?" she asked.

Shaking my head, I whispered, "I can't."

"Let's get out of here and go to my house," she said, rescuing me from the overwhelming tidal wave of too-muchness that was threatening to overtake me.

As we sat on her kitchen counter, the sun streamed across the wood floor. My shoulders relaxed. This was OK; I was OK being with just her, munching on cookies and falling back into our familiar pattern of friendship. I had first met Lauri when my mom was deployed to Kuwait, and she would pray for me when it felt too big for my college freshman shoulders to carry alone.

I started to ask about friends, but I really only wanted to know about Jake. I had fallen in love with him just before my deployment. For the first six months I was in Iraq, we wrote to each other, and when I found a phone every couple of weeks, I would call him. But six months into the war, I felt like a completely different person. I started throwing things away out of fear, and he was one of the things that got thrown out in the trash. I broke up with the guy I loved because I didn't think he could love the person I had become. I was so anxious to see him, but I assumed he must either hold a terrible grudge or have already moved on to someone new. Lauri looked at me quizzically. "Diana, he's not dating anyone; he's waiting for you. He's at church right now."

When that news fully sank in, I scrambled off the kitchen counter, threw the cookie down, and asked, "What are we waiting for?" I pulled Lauri across the street and back to the church building.

Slipping into the back of the sanctuary, I found a chair where I could hide out. The last thing Jake had heard from me after "I love you" was "I'm breaking up with you. Don't write me; don't try to talk to me." I hadn't just broken up with him. I had thrown away a once-in-a-lifetime kind of love. I didn't think there was a way to come back from that.

I slid into the back row during the tail end of the service. The last few people were trickling out of the sanctuary, and my anxiousness to see him after a year apart had me standing up on my tippy toes. While squeezing my hands together nervously, I saw a guy up front with

102

long hair skimming his shoulders. He turned around, flashing familiar twinkling blue eyes. I knew those eyes. I had forgotten that before I'd left for war, Jake and I had promised each other we wouldn't cut our hair until we saw each other again. This med school student who'd had a respectable crew cut when he made this promise was now a man I hardly recognized until his eyes locked on mine. My chest ached with a desperation to be loved. To get back the love I had tried to throw away six months earlier, when the darkness had squeezed out any possibility for good in my life, even him. But here he was, standing in front of me. All I wanted was him.

Before I could think of what to say, my body was drawn toward his six-foot-three frame. Toes almost touching, a millimeter of space and no self-respect between my chest and his, I raised my chin up and caught his blue eyes in mine. I exhaled sharply and blurted, "Can I have a hug?" He looked down at me and, without a word, spread his arms wide open to me. We stepped into the hug as two individuals broken apart, and when we stepped away, something was mended.

* * *

"Bubba, are you awake?" I whispered into the darkness of our bedroom three years later. "I have bad memories that I need to get away from." It was the middle of the night, and half of me was far away, trapped in dusty, terrifying desert places. Clawing my way back to the present, I reached out for the battle buddy I'd never had in that war—the one with whom I now share my life and my name, alongside two little boys. As he'd done a thousand times before, he traveled from his sleep and joined me in my foxhole filled with memories of fear and dread.

Jake and I got married one year after I returned from Iraq, and I began to heal from the trauma of my experience. By our first

103

anniversary, we were pregnant with our oldest son Bridger, and by his first birthday, we were in the process of adopting our second son, Zelalem, from Ethiopia. It was a whirlwind of joy as we became a family. But the scars I could hide under layers of motherhood and work stood out bright white in the moonlight of these nighttime memories.

And so I reached out for my battle buddy. His arms wrapped around me, forming a bridge for me to walk over from the desert sands back into my present. Jake was and is the gravity that held me from spinning out into the atmosphere. When I was displaced, disarmed, and unable to be who I had been when I left, Jake did CPR on my soul. Each day, he coaxed a little more breath back into me, a little more trust in who I was, and belief that whoever I had become through the past year would be accepted. When I returned from the war, my soul was beaten up and beached on an island of pain and confusion. I felt completely alone, except for the man who'd made himself my home before any of it happened. He stands guard over the real me, during the day and when I sleep after waking from a nightmare.

He didn't flinch when our three- and four-year-old children began asking questions about my time as a soldier: "What's war, Mama?" "What kind of guns do they use in war?" "What did you do as a soldier?" "We won, right?" "Why don't you like me to play guns and shoot at my brother?"

Most parents who don't want to talk to their toddlers about death or war can quickly eject themselves out of the conversation with a simple, "I don't know, honey." But I didn't have that luxury. My sons knew I had been a soldier, and they would call my bluff. They'd already found my green duffle bag with the string of numbers painted in black on the side, and they played for hours with the sea of camouflage uniforms with my maiden name stitched on them. Looking into my oldest son's sea-gray eyes with a trickle of green in the center, I'm compelled to tell him the truth as gently as I can. The world is big and beautiful, and he deserves to know how he can build it up or he can break it down with his own two hands or a millisecond tap on a trigger. He will have the honor and the responsibility of this choice every day of his life.

From eating MREs in the desert to making PB&Js for lunch, I was caught between two worlds. Their mom could make them a lightning-quick sandwich on the fly or could disassemble and reassemble a nine-millimeter Beretta blindfolded in under thirty seconds. Over meals at our kitchen counter or while waiting for one of them to finally go potty in their potty chair, we talked—about guns, about God, and about what it means to be peacemakers in our neighborhood, city, and world. I had to find a way to understand these big issues and boil them down to something that made sense to a toddler and to myself. As the saying goes, "If you can't explain something to a child, then you haven't fully grasped it."

When my oldest son was three, we began potty training. We spent long afternoons in the bathroom together, waiting for him to do his business and having some of our longest conversations. He had inherited the ability to stuff every nook and cranny, every moment, with the chatter of his thoughts and questions. He comes by it naturally. Guns had caught his fascination with the strength of the moon's gravitational pull. He wanted to talk about them, read about them, draw pictures of them, and talk about them some more. "What do guns do? What kind of guns do they use in war? What's war, Mama? Why do we war, Mama?"

Looking into his big hazel eyes, I knew one thing. Choosing to give my life away instead of take a life was how I'd found my way

105

back home—to God, to myself, and into the human family. Our only enemies are the things that try to divide us from each other. Self-sacrificing love freed me from having to respond to violence with violence. Faith was no longer a weapon I used to divide "us" from "them"; it became a blank check. As ugly as war is, I needed to tell my son the truth; I couldn't shortchange him with anything less.

"Guns are made to kill," I slowly started to speak. "Anyone who points a gun at someone has to be OK with that person dying."

"So that's why I can't point a play gun at my brother?"

"Yeah. Your creativity is such a gift, and I'd rather see you use it to imagine how to build things up instead of breaking them down."

"Why do they use guns in war then?" For once, my hands weren't trembling when someone mentioned war around me. I could talk to my son about war in a way I couldn't with anyone else. Before our son entered my life, I'd never experienced being wholly myself with zero self-consciousness. He was a magical place for me, like Neverland. I could do anything and everything in his presence. He trusted my goodness in a way only a child can. He gave me wings. I could fly over war memories with him and see them clearly without the pain of them dragging me down to earth, because he hadn't wrapped himself up in the security of war like a blanket. He didn't have a loyalty and allegiance to war as a way of life. He didn't need war, the way most people I knew did.

"War is when two countries disagree and decide to kill each other until the other gives up. That's why war uses guns—because the purpose of war is to kill."

"Oh," he exhaled, "so what gun did you use in the war? And did you kill anybody?" Sheesh, nothing was slowing this kid down; he was like a snowplow in a blizzard.

"I was a medic. I didn't carry the M16 rifle or the big gun you see in pictures, even though I learned how to use those big guns in basic training. When I became a medic, my purpose changed, and so did my gun. A medic protects every life on the battlefield, including enemies. My gun was a nine-millimeter Beretta handgun that was small enough to be strapped to my hip, so I'd have two hands to carry a patient or my medic bag on my back. It was for protecting me or my patient. But it was not a very accurate weapon to kill someone from far away."

Thinking he might have forgotten the second part of his question, I moved toward him to pick him up. "Not done, Mama," he said, extending our potty-training session even longer.

A few minutes later, he launched his question at me again. "Did you kill in the war?" In his questioning hazel eyes, I saw all the little twinkling eyes from the children I'd met in Iraq. Every one of those children had a mama, and I grew up believing I could and should take their lives out of love for myself, my country, and my God. It had all seemed so normal until I looked into my little boy's questioning eyes when he asked, with legs dangling high off the potty, whether his mama had killed another mama's boy. I hated how accurate his question was and how likely it might have been that I would have had to answer him yes.

"No, I thought I had to, but God told me I didn't." I don't know why simple truths are so blurry. Or why it took a war for me to hear the God of love tell me to love my neighbor. But it did. I hoped my son would find his own freedom, that he would never accept anything less than loving his neighbor as himself. I don't claim to understand what that totally means, but not taking the life of a neighbor seems like a beginning. Being his mom made what matters zoom into crystal-clear focus.

My children unlocked things that had been stuck in my throat since the desert days—giving me back my voice and grounding me in my beliefs. They launched me into believing in the goodness of the world again, like a hot-air balloon filling up with so much heat that it rises to the sky with color blazing. It's pure magic.

The wonder of baby cheeks, toddler laughter, and the love that threatened to overwhelm me with its goodness was like surgery on my war wounds. Every day, the wonder of a leaf found or the comfort of curling up to read a book together in the afternoon sunshine healed a part of me. I loved spending bright Saturday mornings together in our house, as sunshine bounced off the honey hardwood floors, lighting up the space.

One morning, the castle of blocks in my son Zelalem's little hands had become a berm for a Hot Wheels car to take off like a jet into the sky. With each push down the ramp, his lips vibrated together, making the engine sound of *brawp, brawp,* bringing the car roaring to life. He exploded with laughter as the car flew like an acrobat in the sky, landing at the end of its flight into the waiting red beanbag chair. His older brother, Bridger, clapped while grabbing the car out of its victory crash pad with his chubby hand. Zelalem snatched the car back from Bridger. In a flash, Bridger's indignant war cry of "Mine!" pierced the air, followed by two fists hammering down onto his little brother's rounded shoulders. Twisting away from the blows, Zelalem screamed while covering the car in his hands, trying to keep his brother from taking it back.

From the kitchen, where I stood, stirring a steaming pot of oatmeal, I heard the laughter turn into screams, which were then interrupted by Jake's baritone voice booming through the cries. "Who did you hit, Bridger? You didn't just hit your brother, you hit *my son.*" The cries died down to small choked-back tears and hiccuped breathing. Tears were running down both sets of brother cheeks. "Do you know why you can't hit your brother?"

Between uneven breaths, Bridger choked out, "Because it's wrong."

Leaning in, laying his larger-than-life hand across his five-year-old's tiny chest, Jake explained, "Your brother is God's son first. That's why you can't hit him. He's not yours to hit. When you hit him, you are hitting someone that God cares so much about that it actually hurts God, too. Do you see how fiercely I am standing up for your brother right now? That's how God feels when anyone is hurt." He swung both boys up onto his lap, drawing them into the crook of each of his arms. Zelalem found comfort in his dad's care while Bridger melted into the arm enfolding him while his legs dangled halfway to the ground. Jake continued, "Why is it wrong to hit your brother, even when he takes your car without asking, Bridger?"

"Because God made him, and I shouldn't hurt things God loves," he murmured, voice muffled as he hid his head in the nook between his dad's chest and shoulder.

"Yes, buddy, I think you've got it. Now you have to make it right with your brother."

I smiled as I spooned brown sugar into the middle of each waiting bowl of steaming oatmeal. Maybe they were getting it. Maybe my sons weren't just hearing me talk about choosing to love even when it's costly. Maybe the way they see their right to hurt another person was actually changing. But would it only play out in our living room, between siblings? Would they choose to love first instead of hit back when it really counted, when it cost them more than being corrected by their dad?

A few weeks later, I waved as my son's tiny legs trudged through the snow, barely moving in his puffy snow pants. "But he hit me!" he exclaimed as he crawled into the backseat of the van. My son was born with his parents' unflagging sense of right and wrong. His face rippled with tears of betrayal and hurt and pure indignant rage. "He punched me, Mom, and then he pushed me down and laughed at me."

"Did you hit him back?" I stammered, as I turned around and pushed his mop of mahogany hair across his forehead, clearing the way to peer into his tear-brimmed eyes. Chin quivering, hiding deep into the collar of his winter coat, he said, "No, because we don't use our hands to hurt someone that God made." Eyes locked on his, Mama Bear anger burning in my stomach at the pint-size bully who had hurt my boy, I swallowed the blind rage. "I'm proud of you, but you know that God's furious right now, right? God loves you so much and doesn't want you to be hurt."

Dropping off my sons at school was now smudged with distrust. The playground used to make me smile as I watched elementary-schoolers pour down the slide and climb back up the other side. Now school was a place where my sons experienced fists from their classmates.

A couple of weeks later, on a sunny Wednesday afternoon, instead of bursting through the door after school, both boys slunk quietly into the house. The quiet was eerie, and I knew something was up. Neither was eager to be the first to tattle—which wasn't normal either. Something had happened, and no one wanted to talk about it.

Finally, my older son, voice shaking, blurted out that his little brother had been called the N-word on the playground that day. My youngest stayed hidden in his room. *He's in kindergarten,* I thought

110

to myself. *Isn't he too young to be wounded by the violence and hate that word carries?*

But he wasn't too young to understand that this wasn't just another name to be called. He did his best to duck and dodge, but he couldn't escape the arrow aimed right at his worth. That day, he was labeled "less than," a label he'd never had to wear before.

Until then, being brown skinned just meant Ethiopian. But now, brown carried shame. It meant other kids on the playground could divide and separate my son from his classmates. It meant he was alone at school. Brown now meant bad.

I hurt for him in a way that made my bones ache. Growing up white, in a white community and family, meant I'd never witnessed how racism could tear into a soul, ripping it into shreds. When Jake and I fell in love in a day, one of the seamless ways we fit together was we both already knew we would have kids who didn't look like us, kids who needed a parent. By the time Bridger was two years old, he was sharing the nursery with our next son, Zelalem, via Ethiopian adoption. We were ignorant of the racism we were bringing him into. I didn't know how it felt to be on the receiving end of bias and hate, which my son had just experienced as a kindergartner.

The world shifted beneath my feet that day. My life as I knew it was now broken into a "before" and "after." This new terrain was terrifying. I had been blind to the insidious ways that racism infects the air we breathe and the water we drink. It was in his school and in us all. Now I saw the threat that had always been there. It shook me. I saw the quick denial in the mom at school who heard about what had happened to my son and said, "Well, kids don't really see color" while holding the hand of her daughter dressed in pink from head to toe. Violence isn't waged only with guns, or war. Words can be violent, and so can the erasure of wrongdoing. As I rocked my son that day, holding his pain was one of the hardest moments of my life.

The weeks rolled into months. Snowflakes dotted the school windows, interspersed with green construction paper Christmas trees dangling from the ceilings. Pulling up outside the school, I took a deep breath before I opened the door to have my two sons tumble out. After that painful incident, leaving them at school felt different. Now it felt like dumping them off at a playground with glass shards hidden in the sand.

I had been struggling to find the right words to say after Bridger was punched and Zelalem was called the N-word. I was busy repairing their little heads and hearts as best as I could at home—handing out warm cookies after school, playing endless rounds of Connect 4, and making each other laugh. But now I needed to tell them something important: "You guys don't hit back when people hurt you with their fists or their words because you know who you are, no matter what. You chose love. Now you know the power you have. I'm in awe of you guys. I could never have done that when I was your age." They nodded their heads at me, shy smiles pasted across their rosy cheeks. I swooped them into a hug before they walked into school. Driving away, I said to myself what I didn't finish telling them but would tell them again and again in bite-size pieces as they grew into themselves: "Now that you have found your freedom to be who you are and choose to love no matter what the circumstances, you are on your way. You just lived your own story. You will build amazing things, restore broken people and relationships, and create beautiful stories. Because that's what love does. The world is incomplete without you. This school, with its good parts and painful parts, our neighborhood, and the world need you both to show up and be yourselves. Be loud. Be curious. Be hurt.

But keep showing up. Because you belong to a family of seven billion people."

Leaving my kids at school that day, I knew one thing. My sons were going to take some hits in life for being peacemakers, but they were going to experience amazing things they haven't even dreamed up yet. Because love is the most powerful weapon on the planet, and they had just learned how to wield it.

11

Preemptive Love

*For unless love becomes tenderness—the connective tissue of love—it never
becomes transformational. The tender doesn't happen tomorrow . . . only now.*
—Gregory Boyle, *Barking to the Choir: The Power of Radical Kinship*

The year before they started elementary school, both my toddler
boys started two days of preschool. After buying them their first
backpacks, I threw a third backpack into the cart and decided to go
back to school myself. I loved being a nurse, but I had always had
my eye on becoming a nurse practitioner, so I could care for patients
independently. As my kids moved toward their school years, I wanted
going back to school to launch me into the next chapter of life.

I enrolled at the College of Saint Scholastica and signed up for
my first classes, including one on public health. For that class, I was
required to write a paper and decided to zero in on issues that had
troubled me years earlier: the conditions affecting the health of the
Iraqi people, and the rumors and reports of heart defects in babies
during the war in Iraq.

In the school library that term, as I was researching my paper, the

115

words *preemptive love* jumped out at me from the computer screen, stopping me in my tracks. While searching for the terms *Iraq* and *health defects*, I stumbled onto a website with a name I couldn't stop rolling around on my tongue: Preemptive Love Coalition. In big, bold text on the coalition's home page, I saw these words: "Violence unmakes the world. Preemptive Love unmakes violence." I shook my head in disbelief, barely noticing the clamor of students studying around me. *Could this be possible?* I whispered to myself. *Can violence be unmade?*

My eyes devoured the website, looking for more clues. Preemptive Love seemed to be living out the love of enemies I had tried to embrace during my deployment. They were seeking out the people who see "us" as the enemy, listening to what those people need, and offering whatever help they could. In Iraq and Syria, this looks like showing up on the front lines of conflict—where the bombs and bullets are still flying—with emergency food, water, and lifesaving medical care. It looks like empowering ISIS survivors and refugees to reclaim their lives from war by creating businesses that give them dignity over dependence. That's what Preemptive Love was doing and still does as an organization: they provide relief and business opportunities for people affected by violence and, in the process, create new stories between communities and people at odds. They recognize that the violence between people who see each other as enemies—Americans and Iraqis, Sunnis and Shias, and Christians and Muslims—needs to be unmade.

This was what Om Hassan had done. She had invited an American soldier into the safety of her home. In doing so, she had crossed over enemy lines and healed my heart from fear. She had walked toward me and chosen to trust me first, even before she knew if I was trustworthy. In loving first, she had unmade the threads of fear and violence between us, our two countries, and our two faiths.

The words of Preemptive Love's tagline, "Healing hearts across enemy lines, beginning with our own," swirled together, tugging on threads from my past and my present. *Even mine?* I whispered.

I wasn't done with my experience in Iraq. I couldn't just turn the page or close the book on that chapter of my life. It had changed me. I knew how to be a peacemaker with bombs and bullets flying, but I didn't know how to do it as a civilian, in my home country, or outside my living room.

A crackle of electricity jolted through my hands. I gathered up the stacks of paper and folders surrounding me, threw them into my backpack, and rushed out of the library. Maybe I wasn't alone in feeling unmade by violence. Someone else must feel it, too, and they were doing work in the same place as I had found the posture of peace—Iraq.

* * *

That evening, after a few hours of feverish research on our home computer, I could hardly wait for Jake to return home with the boys. I heard the van pull up the driveway, followed by little legs moving like molasses. "Come on," I called out the front door, "I have something to show you."

They trudged up the stairs, each step a balancing act of snow boots, backpacks, and art projects. One boy's winter hat had been pushed down so low (by his brother) that it covered most of his eyes. Finally, Jake and I got the boys, snacks in hand, nestled into each of our laps. We sighed, and I clicked the play button to watch Preemptive Love Coalition's TED Talk. "Hi, I'm Jeremy Courtney. I live in Iraq with my family."

"Mama, that's where you lived!" my youngest, Zelalem, exclaimed, his bright ebony eyes looking up at me through thick black lashes.

"You're right, buddy, and I think he has something really important to share with us." Huddled in front of the computer with my husband and children, I knew I wasn't alone.

During the week after we watched the TED Talk, Preemptive Love infected our house. The idea of unmaking violence buzzed in and out of our conversations around the table, on the playground, and during book time. Jake devoured the book *Preemptive Love* in three days and commented about it at breakfast. "You know, I think Iraqis are just regular people," he said through a mouthful of cereal. "I'd like to have them over for dinner." Smiling, I knew he saw it. He had accepted the invitation to reimagine those we've been told are our enemies. Just as I had said yes to Om Hassan's invitation of preemptive love into her house that day, Jake was now seeing Iraqis as his people. Aching with gratefulness, my head found its place, right below his chin in the crook of his neck. Arms wrapping around me, he whispered, "Love you."

The message of the Preemptive Love Coalition put words to the posture Om Hassan had shown me that dusty day in Awaijah. It described what God had asked of me in the war: to be willing to give my life instead of taking a life. It created a new lens of restoration through which to see the violence in my own city and country.

Preemptive Love answered the questions my soul had been asking after finding the posture of peace on the battlefield of Iraq: Now what? What do I do here in my normal life?

How do I lay down my weapon here? How do I choose the other, instead of myself? The answer was simple, but the reality of living it out would change our lives more than we had ever bargained for.

As a family, we decided to blackmail ourselves to love first. This meant that the usual strings we attached to who we showed up for—like agreement, sharing the same faith, politics, or being friends—would no longer apply. Choosing to love first meant everyone would be in our jurisdiction now. No one would be outside of our yes. When a group in our community raised their hand and asked people to show up for them, we would do it.

We decided that we would be the first to love, every single time, because *love never fails.* We were going to throw kindness around like confetti, to love like it was growing on trees, without needing to determine if the person in front of us deserved it or not. This was our family's battle cry. Committing ahead of time to show up with people meant our decision was already made. We stopped talking about what peace might mean and started *being* peace. We did it because peace isn't the absence of conflict; it's showing up in the middle of it.

In the weeks that followed, I couldn't stop myself from emailing the Preemptive Love Coalition. "Dear Preemptive Love Coalition," I began. "I'm an Iraq war veteran, and your belief that we can unmake violence is oxygen to my soul." When I got a reply, it was directly from Jeremy. He said, "Send me your number. I want to call you next week!"

A week later, Jake corralled our kids downstairs while I waited for Jeremy's call from Iraq. When I picked up the ringing phone, I instantly recognized the hum and awkward delay from my first six months in Iraq when I had tried to call Jake, before my low point when I stopped talking to him and everyone else. After a pause, I heard Jeremy's voice: "Hi, Diana. This is Jeremy Courtney calling from Iraq."

"Hello," I stammered into the static. "I just have to tell you, Jeremy, I'm a midwestern mom getting a phone call not only from Iraq but also from someone who I only know from their TED Talk. I'm

119

nervous, because this is wildly outside of my regular Wednesday afternoons."

Laughing, Jeremy said, "I'm really glad to get to talk to you. The whole office in Iraq was so encouraged the day we got your email. You *are* preemptive love, Diana, and I'm honored to meet you. Let me ask you a question: If you could go out on a limb and dream big and do anything with Preemptive Love, what would you do?"

When that call ended, as I walked down the stairs, a thousand thoughts fluttered around my head like butterflies. Bright, darting possibilities carried me down off the tree limb that Jeremy had invited me to climb out onto and dream on. Returning to the familiar cocoon of the living room, where boys sprawled on the floor shooting Hot Wheels cars on a race to the finish, laughter bounced at me, and I smiled. Jake looked up and rushed over to me, tripping over boy legs without breaking eye contact. "So, how did it go?" he asked. "What did he say? What did you say?" Swooping me onto his lap, he plopped us both down on the couch.

"I think he offered me a place at the Preemptive Love table. I get my email account next week, and the Skype staff meeting is on Tuesdays."

Three months after the call with Jeremy, I was perched in the only uncluttered corner of my bedroom trying to find a quiet place in my house to dial up Skype for our Tuesday staff call. My Preemptive Love teammates were peacemakers who chose to stay in Iraq while ISIS invaded the country. They were Iraqis, Canadians, and Americans who were willing to move their families to the place where they believed peace was desperately needed. I looked up to them so much that I had to breathe deeply to keep my voice from shaking when I spoke up. When someone said my name, my head snapped to attention. "Diana, Samford University in Birmingham wants Preemptive Love Coalition to come speak for their forty-five-minute chapel service. Why don't you do it?"

My eyebrows slammed together, as they always do when I am surprised or confused. "Why in the world?" I thought. But then my mouth took the reins and mumbled, "Sure, I'll do it. Where's the script?" The group's response was laughter, which clued me in to a situation I would hear referenced again and again at Preemptive Love: we don't have one; go ahead and create one.

"The most powerful story to tell is your own," Jeremy declared. "Bring your own story to the stage, your own peacemaking journey. That's the story you should tell because it's what the posture of preemptive love looks like."

I had never told my war story to anyone except Jake. I had locked it up tight in the green duffle bag in the basement. My desert conversion to nonviolence was safe within the arms of my little family of four. My sons didn't know who I had been before. They didn't have an allegiance to violence that would make them see me as suspect at best or disloyal at the worst. My family and friends never asked, and I never told. No one asked me if there were bullets in my weapon, so I didn't tell. No one asked whether I would kill a child or an Iraqi, and I didn't tell. No one asked me if my flak vest had bulletproof plates in it, and I didn't tell. No one asked why my sergeant made me sleep next to him, eat next to him, and talk only to him, so I didn't tell. No one asked me why 60 percent of female soldiers deployed to Iraq and Afghanistan reported being sexually assaulted by someone in their chain of command, so I didn't tell about the extra price women paid to serve their beloved country. No one asked. But on the stage at Samford University, I would tell.

* * *

A few weeks later, I stood in the midmorning sunshine while it cast a buttery glow on to the wooden pews in the chapel at Samford University. Students shuffled into their seats and shoved their backpacks under pews. The high-pitched sound of plastic wrappers crinkled through the low buzz of five hundred students. Sunshine streamed through soaring stained-glass windows. The sun-bleached brown of my desert fatigues caught a few eyes, causing murmurs to ripple down the pews. I was certain this was the first time a five-foot female soldier in a battle-bleached desert combat uniform had set foot on their chapel stage. Pumping my fists into my hand to get out the nerves, I prayed for enough courage to speak my story on this stage—because I was done hiding, done trading my battlefield truth for belonging. The price was too high for me.

A Samford student finished introducing me, and before I knew it, my legs were walking me across the wide stage to the small lectern. As I pulled the mic down and smoothed my papers across the stand, the familiar words that I'd practiced for weeks started to swim away from me, and my knees started to knock. Begging my body to cooperate, to breathe in, to form words, I did the only thing left to do: I jumped off the cliff of fear and opened my mouth to speak.

"I flew into the ink-black desert night with my gas mask on and a weapon strapped to my side," I told the students. "We never knew how long we would be deployed; we were never told when we would be able to go home. For 397 nights, I slept in an Iraqi desert tent with a nine-millimeter Beretta lying next to me before I boarded a C-130 cargo plane to return home." My voice marched me to freedom, one sentence, one truth at a time. I stood my ground in the same boots I had stood in while pleading for Baby Muhammed's life to be saved in the desert. This story wasn't about war; it was about how my life had been saved.

When the service ended, a semicircle of ten or so students gathered around the side of the glistening mahogany stage. Each face held something different for me—curiosity from one, beaming pride from another. Standing in the middle of these students who welcomed my story, welcomed me, was like basking in unexpected warm sunshine. It was almost so bright I squinted, not able to see through it all. Each of their smiles brought an electric zap of connection that wiped out my fear and doubts. These people found something beautiful in my story and chose to embrace me.

Breaking through the middle of the semicircle, a girl in a pink shirt marched straight through the open space and set up camp directly in front of me, her arms crossed in front of her. Suddenly, all my survival bells were going off. The way she aggressively broke through the perimeter of the group suggested she was anything but friendly. Staking out the two feet right in front of me, her back to the group, she defiantly locked her gaze on mine.

All eyes, like Ping-Pong balls, bounced to me. Pushing my shoulders back, I looked her brightly in the eyes. Reaching my hand out in front of her, I said, "I'm Diana. What's your name?"

She ignored my outstretched hand, and her voice barreled over me. "You should be ashamed of what you said today—especially wearing that uniform. My daddy's in the army. And I have to tell you how offended and angry I am with what you said up there."

Like a popped party balloon, the camaraderie I had been feeling from the group quickly disappeared. Silence hung suspended in the air, the last bit of oxygen sucked out of the room. Like a sucker punch, shame hit me hard and left my cheeks burning bright red.

I looked her in the eyes and haltingly tried to speak. "I really respect how you had the courage to come up to me and share your feelings. That's hard to do, and I really admire that about you."

She had publicly thrown me under the bus, wanting to cause me harm. She didn't want good for me; in fact, she wanted to shame me. Still, in front of all her peers, I found something about her I could champion, something I could stand alongside of and publicly praise her for. That's what love looks like. It's refusing to be enemies. Love shouldn't turn us into doormats, unable to speak up when injustice happens. True love involves both grace and truth. I gave only grace to the girl in the pink shirt that day. If I had shown her true love, I would have made her aware of the harm she had done to me. She used her words as a stick to strike me, to wound me. And they did.

Violence is a disease, harming everyone it comes in contact with—whether victim or perpetrator, and whether through words or deeds. Love would take the stick out of her hand and say, "This hurts me, and it hurts you." Love doesn't shield us from the harm we cause; it loves us enough to make us aware of it, as James Baldwin says.

When the girl in the pink shirt walked away, another student broke the awkward silence to ask, "You're a third-generation Army veteran. How does your family respond to your peace story?"

"I don't know," I responded. "You guys are the first to hear it."

12

Standing Up for Love and Light

What's the point of having a voice if you're gonna be silent in those moments you shouldn't be?
—Angie Thomas, *The Hate U Give*

"Should we go?" I asked Jake while shoveling broccoli onto a scowling son's plate. Jake's usually twinkling blue eyes were darkened with the seriousness of the decision we were facing: whether to take our boys to the march mourning the murder of Michael Brown, who had been fatally shot by a police officer in Ferguson, Missouri. His death sparked vigils across the country, which intensified when the officer who violently took his life was not indicted. Violence unmakes the world, and we knew that if we showed up, loved first, and mourned with those who mourned, that same violence wouldn't be the end of the story. We heard the pain of Michael Brown's grieving mother, the fear of all the mothers who, like me, are raising brown and black boys in America. When hate is loud, love is not silent. We needed to show up.

"People have been throwing things at marchers in other cities.

People have gotten hurt. I'm scared that if we take them, I won't be able to keep them safe," Jake said in a soft voice.

Hoping little ears were still focused on their plates covered in neon-yellow mountains of mac and cheese, I admitted, "I'm scared, too." Sitting back in my chair, I knew we didn't know what we were doing. I had never been to a vigil or a march in my life. Neither had Jake. We didn't have to do this; we could stay home, read our boys a civil rights book, pray blessings over Michael Brown's mama while tucking them into bed, and call it good. Call ourselves good, our world good, our God good. Part of me wanted to back away from the whole conversation and stop looking outside my magical microcosm of the world—my safe world of little-boy snuggles, naps, and walks to the park.

But I'd heard a mama weep for her baby boy, Michael, and before that, Trayvon's mother and Tamir's. And I couldn't shake it. We were connected to each other. My sons weren't safe until all our children were safe. Listening to his mama on TV beg through tears for America to "say his name," I knew what she was asking. She asked for what every single one of us would beg for: for the world to see the beauty and magic of her son, to say out loud that her son's life mattered. She was asking us to bear witness to her loss, to our loss.

I had decided early on that I wasn't going to shield my children from the violence of this world, because I don't want to shield them from an even bigger reality: light always breaks darkness. Love defies hatred when we stand alongside our neighbors and say, "No more," to violence. I don't want my kids to hold an anemic love in their hands, to feel lost or victimized in a big, scary world. I want them to experience the power that resides in their little bodies and expresses itself in quiet, small words to defy hate and violence.

So we decided to go to the vigil. Standing on the Duluth aerial

126

lift bridge, candles in mitten-covered hands, I looked down into Bridger's bright seven-year-old eyes. "We're going to be OK," I told him through a pinched smile. A scattering of people gathered at the base of the bridge. Signs hung loosely as twenty strangers retied scarves tight and attempted small talk. Tension hung in the air while we waited, knowing that violence against peaceful protestors had been splattered across the news.

Uncomfortable, I looked at the ground, then up at the people holding signs. Scanning the messages on the signs around me: Black Lives Matter; Violence Hurts Us All; White Silence Is Violence; Love Is Greater than Hate; We Love You, Michael. Cold traveled down my spine. I was a fish out of water, here at my first march and vigil for a victim of violence, and it scared me. I had flown halfway around the world and marched across the desert sands into a war. But I had never exercised my citizenship in my own country, in my own city, publicly. Filling in the circles on my ballot every four years was my paltry citizenship in action. Voting couldn't be the sum total of how I exercise my rights as a citizen, but it had been, and I knew it. Standing out here on the familiar main street in my city, I felt exposed and vulnerable. Putting my family's bodies alongside the black community and those mourning Michael felt like putting a target on our backs for those who are fueled by hate and white supremacy. It all felt too public for me.

Someone started singing, "This little light of mine," into the wintry darkness. Voices around me joined in, and we were off. Candles in hand, signs carried like shields, we shuffled across the bridge, singing down the main street. Instead of the bright headlights of cars stopping and going, we carried lanterns and candles, bearing witness and bringing more light into our city. I caught Jake's eye over the top of our two boys sandwiched between us, and tears rolled down my cheeks. Bearing witness to Michael Brown's life put us on holy ground. There was nowhere else to be with my family that night. We were more together and less apart. Sharing shy smiles with those who came to mourn, people from the Black, Indigenous, and LGBTQ communities were all represented in the crowd. So many of the people around us knew what it is like to be ignored, pushed to the margins, and treated as less. They lived solidarity, not letting their differences stop them from showing up for each other. Showing up when violence wounds a community is what love looks like in public. Loving first, with our presence instead of only our prayers, wasn't safe. Laying down my weapon in Iraq wasn't safe either. But it's what you do when you belong to each other.

* * *

The weeks hustled along, as school and our daily routine continued to keep us busy. Even so, we tried to make time to engage with our community more and more. Soon our experiences and new friendships began to have a sort of snowball effect. The Michael Brown vigil was followed by a community breakfast for Martin Luther King Jr. Day, which was followed by learning from our indigenous neighbors. Soon my sons started waving hello and recognizing people they hadn't known before as we continued to show up in our community. What had been unfamiliar and uncomfortable was starting to become OK with us. My sons were being woven into the fabric of our community.

Then three Muslim college kids in Indiana were killed. The news cycle barely registered their deaths, even though they were tied up and shot execution style in their homes. The Muslim Student Association at the small Catholic college perched high on the Duluth hillside of Lake Superior invited the community to grieve the loss of these lives who mirrored their own. Arriving late, I led our family toward the last empty seats, nestling in next to a row of nuns who were the foundation of the school.

"What can we do?" lamented a gray-haired nun to the Muslim student wrapping up the evening.

"Email the parents of the students killed. Tell them their children mattered, and they are not alone."

A nearby voice piped up, "I'm not on the email, but I know how to write letters." The elderly nun sitting next to us who had declared this nodded her chin in determination.

As we walked out of the memorial service that night, I held onto my sons' hands a little tighter, drawing them close. "But why were those boys killed?" Zelalem blurted out.

"Because they were different," I mumbled under the cold night sky. That dreaded "why" question always boomeranged back at me when I didn't quite know how to explain things.

"But how were they different?" Zelalem insisted.

"They were killed because they worship at a different type of church. It's called a mosque." I knew my kids had no idea what a mosque looks like. And I also knew the truth that you can't love a neighbor you don't know. You can't respect how someone else worships God if you've never seen it in action. Grudgingly, I knew what I had to do, even if it felt overwhelming after a heavy night of grieving. Dragging the words out, I said slowly, "Do you want to see a mosque?" I knew their answer before they screeched in unison, "Yes!"

I didn't mention to them that I, too, had never been inside a mosque before. This would be a first for all of us. After a Google search, I found out that our local mosque had a service and welcomed non-Muslims to observe on Friday on the exact same day and time as my sons' school ended that week. We were going.

★ ★ ★

That Friday, after I had picked up my sons from school and driven to the mosque, my hands gripped the steering wheel as I sat in the parking lot, staring straight ahead. If I had been by myself, I would have stayed in the parking lot, too nervous to walk in. But I wanted my kids to know the neighbors they'd been told to fear, to experience relationships instead of separateness. Turning to look at Bridger in the backseat, I caught a hint of his bravery and opened my car door. We held hands while inching across the icy parking lot toward the door. We walked into the entrance and pried off our winter boots to put them in the pile of shoes and boots. A man smiled at Jake and motioned for him and the boys to follow him through the entrance for males up to the service. I stayed with the women.

The service wasn't at all what I had expected. Children gallivanted through the rows of kneeling adults, leaning on random backs like a bird finding a familiar perch to rest on. For the closing prayer, worshippers stretched out their stockinged feet to touch the nearest foot of the neighbor on either side of them. The neat rows of individuals praying were now connected by the zigzag of each person's outstretched feet. As this prayer ended the service, I witnessed the joy of a community celebrating togetherness at the end of the week.

As Bridger, Zelalem, and I gathered with the women in the back after the service, while the men stayed up front talking, a smiling woman named Bridgitte asked me, "Would your boys like a cookie?" I said yes, feeling so grateful to her for taking the first step and talking to me, breaking the ice with cookies and small talk.

When we were back in the car and driving home, I lobbed a question into the backseat: "What did you guys think of the mosque?"

Bridger quickly replied, "I really liked Bridgitte, Mom, and the carpet was *so* soft, and did you see they let kids play and make noise right in the middle of the service?"

"You liked Bridgitte because she gave you three cookies instead of one, Bridger." I knew my sons, and food was their currency of friendship. The moment we walked in, our sons had been surrounded with welcome. I was surprised by how much it moved me to see children so celebrated in a place of worship. I felt wrapped in love just watching these women make a big deal over my shy sons. Now I knew that when my sons heard the word *Muslim* or *mosque*, they would think of Bridgitte, a face instead of just a word. *Muslim* meant something to them now; it meant neighbors and friendship.

* * *

Months rolled into years as the routine of school, piano lessons, and homework shaped our days and rolled us into the next couple of grades. My afternoon routine was marked by a cup of Earl Grey tea; at 2:50 p.m. every school day, I would be in the faded yellow chair by the front window, hands curled around my tea, excitedly waiting for the yellow bus to grind to a halt and return my favorite little people to me. Like a puppy, I would plant myself in the yellow chair we'd bought for our first baby's nursery and wait excitedly, exhaling the peacemaking work I did with Preemptive Love Coalition and inhaling to prepare for sticky hugs, Uno games, and the party that filled the house when these two tumbled off the bus and back into my arms.

But one day, when winter stretched out its shadow, draping our days in early darkness, I was more worried than excited. I'd been watching reports of the nightclub shooting in Orlando that had left fifty dead—most of them Hispanic and members of the LGBTQ community, making this the deadliest incident of violence against LGBTQ people in history. What should I tell my kids? I didn't want violence and death to puncture their elementary-school balloon of bliss.

A vigil for the victims was scheduled to take place in our city that evening. The LGBTQ group asked the Duluth community to join them and mourn together. When a group raised their hand and asked to be seen or heard, we had already given our yes. We would be there. I didn't have to know how to explain everything. Choosing to love had been the way I found my freedom in the desert. I couldn't give my kids anything less than that same freedom.

As soon as the boys came in the door and sat down for a snack of crackers and carrot slices, I worked up the courage to just say it: "So, after dad gets home from work tonight, we're going to a vigil."

White flecks of saltines clung to the corners of Bridger's mouth as he chewed. His eyebrows jumped together, digging for the meaning of the word *vigil*. "Like when the candles come out?"

"Yeah, buddy, like when we lit candles for the boy who died—Michael."

"Oh, OK. Do you think they'll have enough candles for everyone this time?" he asked in an earnest voice. As the oldest, he has a keen eye for fairness; nothing escapes his watchful gaze.

"Who got hurt this time, Mama?" Zelalem chirped. My youngest notices people and loves people in a superhero-type way for being so small. He is our canary in the coal mine, noticing before anyone else when people aren't OK.

"Some people were killed in Orlando, Florida," I responded.

"But why, Mama?" I took a breath and knew I had to try to answer him. "I don't really know the whole reason why, buddy, but the people all had something in common. They were in a place where men who love men and women who love women gather together. It was supposed to be a safe place for them, a place where they could be themselves without fear. Outside of this place, they often have experienced fear and sometimes being hated for who and how they love."

Guilt gnawed at my belly. I had a complicated history with the LGBTQ community. The faith cards I was dealt were absolute and damning for the LGBTQ folks. If the church in which I had grown up had had a list of "the other," the first entries on that list would have been people who were pro-choice or pro-LGBTQ. Being gay was so looked down upon that even having anything to do with someone who was gay could have been seen as a direct challenge to my "loyalty" to God. I wouldn't have been caught dead near an LGBTQ meeting—not because I feared God, but because I feared my faith group. I was scared that someone in my faith community would snatch my Jesus card away and take away my belonging.

* * *

That evening, at the vigil, the bell rang fifty times, once as each victim's name rang out over us. Each time, the sound hit the shoulders of the half-moon-shaped group of mourners with a thump of grief. The moment of silence between each clang of the bell was our way to honor the lives lost. These lives weren't lost from disease or an accident. They were taken by intentional violence. Murdered. Terror rippled through their last breaths, screams echoing above the rat-tat-tat of the automatic-gun fire. I knew that sound well. I knew how it felt to be scared with bullets ripping around you.

Biting my lip, I inched back the pain that brimmed up, pooling in as story after story was read from the microphone by people who experienced discrimination for growing up Queer or because they were raised by someone who was. "I was teased and hated in school, not because I was gay but because I had two moms who were." "Going to a gay club was the first place I felt safe, first time I felt like I was myself." Each story wove the same thread: the fear of rejection and violence and how clubs like Pulse had been a safe haven from it all. Waves of human pain, and even laughter in the middle of the tears, washed away my fear of what people in my faith community would think of me for being there. I knew I might be judged or excluded for publicly standing alongside the LGBTQ community. But love was my life's battle cry, the truth I had blackmailed myself into living, no matter what, no matter where. Love was my North Star, and it had led me here.

The shooter's violence was part of my unspoken violence—violence that grows out of not seeing our humanity as tied up in the humanity of those we are taught to call enemies. Surrounded by all of these brave stories and beautiful love, my hidden places of years of indifference and ignorance throbbed. It hurt to understand how my ignorance of the violence done against people in this community made the world even more unsafe for them. Proximity to their pain scrubbed my ignorance raw. The opposite of love is never hate, it's always indifference. Because indifference erases and accepts the violence done against another person.

When the speakers had finished, we lit the candles. Each person passed the flame to the person next to them. Light leaped across the semicircle, pushing back darkness and making the eyes of every person holding a candle come alive. Squeezing Jake's hand, I watched through my tears as he picked two rainbow ribbon pins out of the basket being passed around.

Stepping in front of each son, he knelt down, locked eyes on them, and held the ribbon in his palm out front at eye level. "If you choose to wear this ribbon," he said to them, "it means you are no longer putting yourself first. And it will cost you. You are telling the world, everyone you meet, that the lives of LGBTQ people are just as important as your own, that violence against them is violence against you. You are standing up and alongside of anyone who loves differently and saying they deserve to be safe and valued. People you don't even know might call you names and yell at you because you are wearing this ribbon. It's your choice; you don't have to wear this ribbon. But if you do, I want you to understand what it means and what you are saying yes to. Do want to wear this ribbon?" Their eyes bounced to each other, and then their heads nodded an emphatic yes. Watching Jake pin ribbons onto their chests broke the dam of tears I'd been holding back. He was pinning love onto these little chests. He had knighted them for love instead of indifference.

I saw through tears that this was their baptism, mirroring my own desert baptism. Just as my choice not to prioritize my own life over the life of an Iraqi child had the potential to cost me everything, my sons' choice could cost them—their social standing, their feeling of easy belonging or acceptance, or even their safety. Laying down their right to put themselves first was like going down into a watery grave. But rising out of this choice was a life of love, a free life, a life of giving instead of taking. Indifference and the fear of being judged burned out like a flame without oxygen, replaced with an overflowing solidarity. Loving first is costly, but there isn't any other way to love.

* * *

135

Days rolled into weeks until spring marched us into the last months of the school year. Each school year ended with a bang when every teacher who had invested in our sons, from kindergarten through fifth grade, came over for a barbecue and bocce ball party to celebrate them. Usually it was the kickoff to a summer bursting with possibilities of parties and long lazy days in the sun.

But the end of this school year felt different: this year had ushered in crises and divides that overshadowed the coming summer days. I'd never seen anything like it before. The news headlines reported people running for their lives and leaving their homes and countries behind as violence pushed asylum seekers and migrants across deserts and to the US–Mexico border. Conversations had been bouncing across our dinner table about what the children in this situation might be feeling. How could we help when we were so far away?

At the same time, moving ourselves toward trying to be peacemakers in our community ended up moving us to another place to worship. We kept seeing a few faces that showed up rain or shine for those on the margins in our community. When I asked around, I found out that they worshipped at the same place. "Peace Church has been a faithful friend to us for over twenty years," I heard from friends at the historic African American church we attended off and on for events. I needed a soft spot to land where God and violence weren't intertwined and where worshippers raised their hands to God without raising their children to be willing to take another's life for their country. I wanted to sit and learn from people whose faith created a weekly rhythm of feeding and feasting with neighbors on the margins. I ached to see a different way people lived out their faith. I needed to heal, and this church was a soft place for me to land.

Peace Church was participating in a Lights for Liberty event that aimed to set aside a Friday night on which people across the United

States would gather to light candles and acknowledge the children and families at the border, to remember the children who had been detained and the ones who had died. The event, put on by Faith leaders and activists, included listening to community members' stories of being an immigrant and having family still in Mexico, as well as learning what being an American in this situation might require from us.

The Preemptive Love Coalition didn't show up only for refugees in Iraq and Syria. They also showed up at the US-Mexico border with support for asylum seekers as they ran for their lives from violence. Speaking for Preemptive Love usually meant leaving my family and boarding a plane to be with new people. But Peace Church had asked me to speak at its Lights for Liberty event, and being asked to speak in my home church and home community was really special.

The night of the event, I stood in a front pew of the darkened church, listening to the singing of my community around me. My family plus my two nephews sat next to each other, taking up a whole pew. I felt a nervous hope percolate. Looking around at the sea of faces behind me, I saw more kids than I've ever seen at these community events. My sons smiled and whispered-yelled as each spotted a friend from school and waved hello. Speaking up is brave, and speaking up when it's about a wrong in your own country is terrifying. I couldn't believe how many brave parents had brought their kids to Lights for Liberty.

"Good luck, Mom," Zelalem whispered as he nudged me to look at the drawing in his lap. It was of a heart with me in the middle with a microphone. He always knew how to sneak courage into my hands right when I needed it. It was an honor to carry stories of vulnerable people who deserve to be seen and cared for. But I always got butterflies in my stomach before public speaking, and he knew it.

I took a deep breath and reminded myself why I wasn't willing to be silent anymore. I had promised myself that when people were being hurt, I would speak up. I did it so my sons would see and embrace their own power to speak up for those who are vulnerable. I did it so people who have felt unseen would know they are not alone. I didn't want anyone to be erased because who they are doesn't fit the narrative people have made about them. I myself have struggled to find my voice in all the narratives I didn't fit. I was a white mother raising a black son and a white son, a peacemaker who has waged war, a soldier who was a female combat veteran, a Christian who won't accept violence done for my benefit or done against my indigenous, black, Muslim, and LGBTQ neighbors.

Standing on the stage with my heart pounding, I took a deep breath and caught the eyes of my family. "Soldiers fight for freedom outside of our country," I began, "so who fights for liberty and justice *inside* America? We do. And you are tonight. Thank you for showing up for our neighbors at the border."

What I didn't say out loud that night was that I wasn't compelled to speak only for the Preemptive Love Coalition. Rather, my conscience as a soldier had pushed me up to the microphone. The day I had been deployed for active duty to Iraq, the distance between my country's policies and the people affected by those policies evaporated. I couldn't feel any space between how my country was treating human beings at the border and my complicity in it. As a soldier, I had pledged to a code of honor, and part of that code defines how we treat our enemy, POWs, and civilians. Further, in basic training, when they taught us what to do if we were captured by the enemy, I was terrified, and the only thing that tamped down my fear was the rules of war in the Geneva Convention. It required our enemy to give us rights like food, safety, medical care, and the ability to communicate with our family or country about where we were being held. We carried a copy of the Geneva Convention in our uniform's left pocket.

From that perspective, it broke my wartime code of honor to hold children and families in inhumane conditions and to separate family members without information about where each other was. And this was happening in peacetime, on my own soil. If I hoped my enemy would honor the Geneva Convention and give me basic rights while I was warring against them, how could my country not give these basic rights to people who weren't even enemy combatants but were scared mothers and fathers running from violence with their children in tow? For me, this wasn't politics; this was about people. It's shouldering the responsibility of being an American. I didn't know what to say or how to say it. But I needed my boys to see that you speak up when you see something that needs to be fixed, even when wrong is being done by people you love or the country you love.

So at the Lights for Liberty event, I said, "We don't have to agree on immigration, border security, politics, or faith to link arms and say that detention centers on our soil are not a reflection of who we want America to be or the kind of legacy we want to hand down to our children. Dehumanizing our brothers and sisters at the border comes with a high cost. It will cost us liberty, because injustice anywhere is a threat to justice everywhere. No matter who we are—mothers, fathers, or young people—we *know* when we see a wrong that needs to be righted. The choice is whether we will have the courage to speak up and confront those we love—our friends, our neighbors, and our own country.

"I believe our children are counting on us, watching to see what we do right now," I continued. "We have a road map from our elders and ancestors who have shown us how to shine light when our country is in the deepest night. We have the love of MLK Jr. to guide us, the power of Fannie Lou Hamer, the quiet revolution of Rosa Parks sitting, Colin Kaepernick silently kneeling, and Senator John Lewis's persistence, running for Congress after being beaten and jailed for trying to vote. We are ready for this."

Ending the speech, I walked off the stage toward four grinning elementary-school boys hanging over the pew, giving me big thumbs-up signs and lopsided grins. "I knew you could do it!" Zelalem whispered as I squeezed myself in between him and Jake, finding my place under Jake's comforting arm.

13

Dr. Sabah

When one of us is cut, we all bleed. This is humanity.
—Sabah Alwan

Nervous to be knocking on a stranger's door on a wintry Saturday afternoon, I had been sitting in my car for a few moments, breathing and trying to dig up some courage to propel me out of my car and to his door. I didn't know who he was, and he certainly didn't know anything about me. I wondered what kind of person would say yes to a stranger who had emailed his university, asking for someone to provide an Arabic translation. Being a peacemaker for Preemptive Love Coalition propelled me into unique situations, but this was a first. Taking a deep breath, I opened the car door. Walking up to the home, I spotted a bright brass door knocker inscribed with the words "Dr. Sabah Alwan, established 2005." At least I was knocking on the correct stranger's door, I mumbled to myself.

"Come in, come in, and take your shoes off." The man's green eyes sparkled as he whisked me into his home. Taking my shoes off, I followed him up the stairs to a plush couch in the living room. Bright blues, reds, and yellows dotted the pillows on the couches, metal lamps dangled from the ceiling, streams of purple ribbons wrapped with green ribbons hanging down like crepe paper decorations. The colors here were not the usual beige and white that most homes in my city wore like a standard uniform. Silver sabers, locked across each other, hung on the wall above the dining room table where the white dish sat filled with pink and green fennel seed candy, a Middle Eastern staple.

"Espresso or tea?" he asked as his jovial eyes smiled. "My wife makes an amazing cup of either."

"Tea." I smiled back at him.

"You look familiar," his wife, Caterina, said. "You were at the Muslim student memorial service with your kids, right?" She was too polite to mention that I had been the one who interrupted the whole service by coming in late with kids who whisper-screamed their questions to me during the service, and who double-dipped at the refreshments table just enough to have the hummus bowl to themselves at the end of the night.

Returning from the kitchen, Dr. Sabah held two glasses of steaming Arabic tea. Each short, slim, ornate glass sat in the middle of a clear saucer, with a spoon standing up in the middle of the tea glass like a flagpole. He handed me one glass, and hoping to discover how to drink it before I spilled it, I lowered the tea onto the coffee table in front of me, noticing another set of sabers lying underneath the glass tabletop. Stirring the tea with my spoon, I found that the bottom third of the glass seemed to be cemented in white sugar. Looking up, I saw Dr. Sabah raise the glass to his mouth with the spoon standing in it, not lying on the side of the saucer. I confidently tried to take my first sip in the same way, but the spoon stabbed the edge of my nose with a sting, stopping my glass from getting to my mouth.

"Oh," he said, surprised, "you can take the spoon out if you need to." Trying to recover and distract from my flaming red cheeks, I asked him where he had learned Arabic. "Iraq," he said, pronouncing the *q* in the lilting way no American I knew ever could. His eyes lit up, while his body seemed to vibrate with energy I didn't expect, based on his gray hair and his position as a behavioral-science professor. "I grew up in a suburb of Baghdad. It's so beautiful there—the lush green gardens, the fruit trees, watermelons, the Euphrates River and the Tigris."

"I know." I leaned forward with excitement. "I've seen the Euphrates gushing at dusk, the city of Ur's ziggurat at dawn. Too stunning for words."

Sharing memories of Iraq's beauty—Babylon and its Hanging Gardens, the outsize watermelons and cantaloupes—is something I hadn't done with anyone since leaving Iraq. We reminisced about the side of Iraq the media neglects to show: gardens, mountains of melons stacked up, neighborhoods going about the daily routine of walking to school, and street soccer games. The way the sunlight melts at sunset makes ordinary buildings shimmer.

"How did you come to see my country?" he asked, his lively green eyes locking onto mine.

"I was deployed in 2003 as a medic in the Iraq War. I was part of the preemptive strike," I said quietly, eyes traveling down into the half-empty tea glass in my lap. The joy of sharing the beauty of his homeland screeched to a halt. I wasn't sure how he felt about serving tea to someone who had invaded his country, uninvited. The American invasion had left a wake of civilian violence and destruction. We both had been told we were each other's enemy.

I didn't have the courage to lift my eyes back up to meet his. I knew how much of his beloved country was in rubble. The silence between us might be the last calm before he showed me the door and read me the riot act. Part of me might feel less tension if he would.

With the slightest perceivable motion, he nodded. He had heard me. "I always wanted to go back," he said quietly. Then, as if I hadn't blurted out my confession, he continued, "I never planned on staying in America after I got my education."

Dr. Sabah had left Iraq when he was nineteen years old. He had wanted to be a doctor, but he wasn't one of the few students accepted into Iraq's one and only prestigious medical school, so he came to the states and got his PhD in behavioral sciences. That was thirty years ago. "For years, every time I tried to go back to my home, some act of violence would make it impossible."

He added, "I did go back when my mother was sick with cancer. I went home to take care of her." By that time, the United States had imposed strict sanctions on Saddam's regime. Many Iraqi families struggled to find food. Caterina, Dr. Sabah's wife, recalled their time there. "I had just had our first baby—she was six weeks old—and I went to be with Sabah while his mother was sick. My own mother said I was crazy to go. I lost forty pounds in a month, because there wasn't enough food to eat." Caterina learned a new expression from the shopkeepers—*makkah*, meaning "nothing"—while she searched the markets for food to buy.

Dr. Sabah glowed while describing the majesty of Iraq before it was engulfed in war. "At one time, Iraq graduated more PhDs per year than any other country—and I mean women as well as men," he proudly clarified with his finger wagging in the air. As a father of two girls, he cares deeply about their value and wants them to have every educational opportunity. "We had one of the most state-of-the-art medical systems," he continued. "Western countries were looking at Iraq's model of care." All that was before the first Gulf War in 1991—the Bush-era bombings.

"After that, we had nothing. Every building over four stories tall was bombed. That meant our hospitals were gone. My mother was given the wrong type of medicine for her cancer, because that was all they had left on the oncology ward. This made her sicker." His voice cracked, and pausing, he looked away. "She suffered horribly. Cancer without pain medicine," he said, tears rolling down his cheeks, "is an unconscionable way to die." He shared some of the other devastating effects of war that he had witnessed. "The bombings destroyed our sewer system, so we were infected with disease." He stopped, quietly found my eyes, and held them tightly. "These are crimes against humanity, Diana."

I couldn't break free from the sharp edges of the pain-filled truth I witnessed when I gazed into his eyes. I breathed deeply and pleaded with myself not to get up or turn away. If Dr. Sabah had to watch his mother die in horrific pain, I could stay here with him. I could witness his pain without trying to duck and cover from the pain it brought up in my own mind and heart. It *was* a crime against humanity. All of it was—his pain and mine. Wet tears rolled down his face, even though we were speaking more than a decade after his mother's death. Pain is the most agile time traveler.

In that moment, we weren't the Iraqi professor and the American soldier. We were just people, sitting with each other's raw loss.

At last, his soft, fatherly eyes settled on me, and he asked, "How could they send a twenty-three-year-old woman thousands of miles away to wage war in a country she knew nothing about?" What he was kind enough not to say was that I had been sent to wage war, not just in a country I knew nothing about, but in a country I *cared* nothing about. And that painful truth hung in the air between us.

145

"I don't know," was all I could choke out through a burning throat, holding back tears. To be honest, I still don't have an answer.

Memories poured over me—the fear I had felt as the plane touched down in Iraq, charging into the ink-black desert night, stumbling across a gleaming white skull in the desert, trying to avoid stepping on old land mines left in the sand, listening to the news of who died each day as if it were the weather report, the "new normal" of being shot at every day. I couldn't make any sense of it.

Thirteen years later, sitting on Dr. Sabah's couch, surrounded by bright Middle Eastern pillows, I still couldn't. But I knew I had a choice. I could choose to remind Dr. Sabah that I had been ten years old when Bush was elected and therefore really held no responsibility for the pain rolling down his wet cheeks. Or I could remove my bulletproof plates, lay them down in the sand, and allow his pain to make me bleed, too.

Self-protection was my knee-jerk reaction, to dodge pain, but I had found a different way to live, one that had brought me back to life on the battlefield and given me a posture to move through my everyday life. I wasn't serving the master of self-protection anymore. I already had counted the costs, and me-first living was too great of a weight to bear. When I had released all fifteen bullets out of my nine-millimeter Beretta magazine in the darkest desert night my soul had ever known, I had been choosing Dr. Sabah over myself. I had already made the choice not to run and not to defend myself against his pain.

Turning toward him, through bleary eyes, I said in a quivering voice one of the hardest things I've ever said: "Tell me more."

Dr. Sabah and I sat with the weight of our collective human pain and confusion between us. We didn't have answers. We didn't choose loyalty to country over people. We didn't turn away. We acknowledged the suffering and loss that had taken place on Iraqi soil. We acknowledged the wounds many American soldiers carry to this day.

Dr. Sabah taught me you don't have to demonize others in order to grieve your own pain. He showed me that he can mourn the bombings and bullets in Iraq and still offer love to his American neighbors. He chose preemptive love before he ever opened the door to a stranger with hidden war wounds.

Dr. Sabah leaned toward me first. He remade part of my unfinished soldier story and challenged me to continue my unfinished human story. The day I left Om Hassan in the village, I thought that would be the last time I would ever be invited into an Iraqi home as a friend. Sitting on Dr. Sabah's couch, watching his teenage sons walk past him and plop a kiss on his cheek, felt as if I found something I had lost.

Dr. Sabah saw me that day—not just the uniform I had worn or the country I am from. He saw my cuts, and he chose to bleed with me.

The afternoon turned to evening; my one-hour visit snowballed into three, when my phone buzzed with texts from Jake: "Are you OK? Where are you?" Like Jake, I never imagined what I would find by knocking on a stranger's door for an Arabic translation.

As Dr. Sabah found his pen and, like an artist painting on a canvas, started translating the English words into the stunning slants and intricate slopes of Arabic, the conversation turned to families. "I have three sons and two girls," he commented as he showed me the finished translation.

"Wow, how hard was it raising Muslim kids in Duluth?" I asked.

"Not as hard as it will be for you raising your black son here," he declared without looking up from cleaning his calligraphy pens. Dr. Sabah knew what I didn't. He knew what it means to have his kids

147

be seen as outsiders, for their names to raise red flags and them to be seen as suspicious. Long after the sun had set, as I walked out of his house, he waved at me with his prayer beads in his hand and yelled, "Bring your family over for dinner. Caterina is an amazing cook!"

* * *

After that first meeting, Dr. Sabah embraced my family. He understood what it is like to be treated as not fully welcomed or trusted. He knew more than I did that my younger son's stunning ebony skin would be a lightning rod for violence and hate in middle school and high school. I shuddered when I listened to the stories Dr. Sabah told.

Before long, his dinner invitation materialized, and all four of us were gathered around his table. He and Caterina had a way about them that invited my sons directly into the center of conversation and friendship. "Boys! Come meet our guests," Dr. Sabah yelled as his twin teenage boys barreled through the front door. Walking into the living room, each son bear-hugged his dad before looking up to see who else was in the living room. Sabah's green eyes twinkled as he planted a big kiss on each of his son's cheeks; sheer joy beamed out of him. Dr. Sabah offered that same alchemy of bold delight and familiar welcome to my sons. I watched them respond with full-throttle affection I'd rarely seen them display even to family, much less someone they saw only a few times a year.

As the months passed and we saw headline after headline of unarmed black boys and men being killed, I'd get a message from Dr. Sabah, asking how we were holding up. It was reassuring to know that he saw my family and was in our corner. I didn't need to bring it up or carefully explain why the headline felt like a sucker punch. He understood.

His friendship rooted me and helped me weave my past back into my present. It wasn't only that he was from Iraq or that we were a Christian and a Muslim who laughed at each other's stories until our cheeks hurt. He saw me. He was the first person to look me in the eye and question why I had been sent to war, the way I imagined a protective father would do. He honored me as a peacemaker because he was a man of peace. He knew violence, and he knew the cost of peace. He believed in the value of humanity more than he believed in blind loyalty to countries. As different as we were, we found ourselves fellow countrymen in our commitment to love.

* * *

One Thursday night, my phone buzzed on my nightstand. It was Ihsan, a colleague from the Preemptive Love Coalition, calling from Iraq. Although we hadn't met during that time, we had both lived through the invasion of 2003 in the same part of Iraq, his home province. His village was one over from my base. That shared experience became the basis of our unlikely friendship when I joined the staff of Preemptive Love.

Ihsan was calling to tell me about the New Zealand mosque shooting, which had just taken more than fifty lives while they worshipped. Lying in bed, slowly taking in how hate had once again hurt people I loved, I didn't want to make room for peace. I hated this violence.

"I am so sorry, Ihsan. How are you doing? How is your family?" I stammered into my phone, using the app that allowed us to communicate in real time across the time zones.

"I don't know, Diana, I am afraid for my family, for all Muslims going to worship and pray tomorrow. I can't believe we aren't safe in the place we go to pray to God." Friday is the day of the week when the Muslim community comes together to pray. Would anyone feel safe enough to go tomorrow? To take their children?

I didn't know what to say or what I should do, but I knew one thing. When hate is loud, love cannot be silent. When I got off the phone with Ihsan, Dr. Sabah was one of the first people I messaged. "I'm so sorry for the violence that happened. We love you and your family. How are you doing?"

The next day, my kids and I went to the mosque before the Friday prayers started. We tied signs to the entrance. The messages "We Love Our Muslim Neighbors" and "Love Wins" would greet those who braved coming to pray that afternoon. Candles and flowers sat in the snowbank, honoring the Muslim lives taken in New Zealand, while bright balloons wrapped around the columns of the entrance, celebrating our neighbors who worship here. In sidewalk chalk, Bridger scrawled, "We love you," while Zelalem, always the artist, drew big swooping hearts. This place would be marked by love instead of hate.

The trickle of people who arrived to pray were astonished by the tiny group of neighbors waiting to welcome them with smiles and hugs. "Come in, come in," urged the president of the mosque. Even in grief, hospitality was abundant. My kids and I joined the worship service. We walked in and put our shoes on top of the pile. I noticed a large chain padlocking the front doors closed. The lock was on the inside, not the outside, reminding me that not everyone was safe to practice religion in my city. Some of my neighbors had to lock their doors while they worshipped.

While we walked into the service, others stood outside, holding vigil. Their intent was to make the mosque safer that day by putting their bodies in front of it.

At the end of the service, we stood shoulder to shoulder. "This prayer is to honor those killed," the woman next to me whispered. Looking over at my sons' faces, I searched for evidence that this grieving was too much for their little hearts. I didn't find what I had thought I would. Their faces looked relaxed, and their shoulders were already touching mine and those of the person next to them. Holding candles at vigils didn't seem to dim their trust and hope in the world. They walked out of these events brighter, as if the community gathering together lifted the darkness and left them more confident that a community that loves loud is stronger than any violent act.

We entered the mosque grieving and left with something different: hope. This is the power of presence, of proximity instead of separation. In joy or pain, the smiles and hugs reminded us that belonging together is what makes us strong. We aren't alone.

On the sidewalk outside the mosque, we slowly said good-byes and walked to our car. Naeem, the president of the mosque, hustled toward us. He wrapped his arms around my sons and me. "Thank you for being with us," he choked out, "especially today." As we stood together, he added with tears in his eyes, "There is so much misunderstanding of Muslims. If there is anyone in your circles who doesn't understand who we are, that we are people of peace, I'm here to talk with them. I'd like to get to know them."

Walking away, I didn't understand how he had the strength to stand with his hands open like that. Even though his religion was targeted by violence, he took the burden on himself to reach out to those who refused to see him as a neighbor. Naeem was patient, Naeem was kind, Naeem was not self-seeking. He cared more for others than himself. He refused to keep a record of wrongs. Naeem was love.

★ ★ ★

Less than two months later, I got a phone call from Dr. Sabah. "Come before sunset, and you can break the fast with us," he said. It was his holiest month of Ramadan, a time of spiritual introspection, of fasting—feeling hunger to remember those who hunger—and a time of drawing near to God. The month of Ramadan meant his family and all my Muslim friends and colleagues would be going about their days—going to work, caring for their children, living their lives—all without food or water. Eating would happen only before sunrise or after the sun went down. I couldn't imagine it. Most holy days in my faith meant extra helpings of food, not fasting; gifts, not spiritual disciplines; and a family-only meal instead of inviting friends outside the faith. I had never been invited to celebrate Ramadan before, and I knew what a special gift it was for a friend to invite us into one of the holiest and hardest times of their faith.

We gathered outside in the dusky evening, enjoying the spring air and telling stories until the sun dropped below the tree line. As we sat together, I was caught off guard by the lump growing in my throat. Watching my children bask in Dr. Sabah's exaggerated storytelling filled me with so much joy that tears misted in my eyes.

When the sun set, Dr. Sabah stood up and announced, "It's time to break the fast." As I stood in the kitchen, chatting with Caterina as my family helped pour the first course, a clear soup, into bowls, I caught my sons watching Dr. Sabah practice his devotion to God, standing in his living room, facing east, with his sons standing behind him, heads bowed, hands together. The words moved them in unison: on their knees, foreheads touching the ground, and back to standing. For the second time that evening, tears filled my eyes. My children were seeing the beauty of Islam and the beauty of the people of Iraq firsthand.

My sons grew up hearing about Iraq like a fabled story: the place I traveled *to*, believing in enemies and violence as the way to make the crooked world straight, and the place I returned *from*, holding only love instead of a weapon. It was a powerful, magical place that they couldn't touch, visit, or join in. Instead, they were relegated to listening to old stories and sitting on the sidelines. Being unable to share the Iraqi experience and friendships I had made with these three important people made me ache.

Turning to look at my sons, I smiled as I watched them sparkle with laughter under Dr. Sabah's spell, touching and tasting and finally seeing the goodness of Iraq for themselves. We were supposed to be enemies—Americans and Iraqis, Muslims and Christians, newer immigrants and historical immigrants. But here we were, huddled around the table together, with candlelight flickering off cheeks and smiling eyes.

The world dismissed and distrusted each of us for different reasons—being a Muslim, having dark skin, being a Christian who refused violence, or using the lilting accent of an immigrant. All these things were used by others like crowbars to peel us away from belonging. But as I saw the candles light up the faces around the table, the darkness didn't seem so dark. These people sat shoulder to shoulder, choosing each other. We belonged to each other.

We were outsiders, yes, but insiders to a hard-won truth: Giving your life away is the only way to truly find it. Loving our enemies is what transforms fear into freedom. Love has the power to change us. As Dr. Sabah told me that first day over tea, "When one of us is cut, we all bleed. That is humanity."

14

Return to Iraq

How many feelings can one heart hold?... Infinite, Luna thought. The way
the universe is infinite. It is light and dark and endless motion; it is space and
time, and space within space, and time within time. And she knew: there is no
limit to what the heart can carry.
—Kelly Barnhill, *The Girl Who Drank the Moon*

From the moment I found out the Preemptive Love Coalition was
based in Iraq, I clung tightly to a dream of going back. If I returned
with Preemptive Love, I would be waging peace instead of waging
war. I couldn't even put words to what ricocheted in my chest when
I thought about it. Like lightning across the sky, it felt electric and
terrifying. I wanted it. And I feared it.

I wouldn't be the first veteran to return to the place where they
had waged war. Veterans from wars before mine—Vietnam War vets
and World War II vets—are inexplicably drawn back to the countries
where they had waged war. Some call it paying their respects. I think
it's more personal than that. To stand on the soil that changed you is
to bear witness to a truth.

But it is scary as hell to try to put your hands on a time and a place that might not be real anymore. What if it slips through my hands like water? By revisiting the past, we have an opportunity to see ourselves more clearly in the present, and we don't always know what that vision will reveal. We hope and pray that we will experience something good, not a hurricane of hopelessness, pain, or regret. It's like reaching for the hand of the person you love, hoping to feel the electric chemistry that brought you together instead of the pain of past fights. But the biggest fear is that when you grab their hand, you won't feel anything at all.

After years of hoping I would be asked to go back to Iraq, it finally happened. I opened the card at the Preemptive Love yearly staff summit that said, "Thank you for working so hard for our refugee friends, Diana. In honor of your three years working here, we would like to invite you to come see the work that you've helped make possible in Iraq. Pack your bags!" I was going to get to meet our refugee friends whose story I'd been telling to people across the US for years. I felt like I knew them, but this would be the first chance for them to know me. I would get to sit in homes and see the businesses that have changed our Iraqi and Syrian friends' lives. I couldn't wait.

* * *

Two weeks before I was supposed to leave for Iraq, I wasn't sure I could go through with it. In my head, I wanted to board the plane, but my heart beat fast when I thought about it. I wondered if my body's traumatic memories of getting onto a plane headed for war would make my legs freeze up on the Jetway. What if my head was fine but my body's survival instincts wouldn't let me walk onto the plane?

The underlying thrum of these fears brought me to Dr. Sabah's office. I wasn't sure what I needed. Sitting down across from his desk, I looked around, waiting for him to come in, admiring the wall hangings covered in black Arabic text and the windows draped with the bright splashes of color that announced Middle Eastern flair. As my eyes wandered among his multiple diplomas and award certificates, I found a frame containing a faded piece of paper: a crayon drawing of a stick boy and a stick dad holding hands, with the name of his son, now in college, scrawled in the corner.

"Diana!" exclaimed Dr. Sabah as he walked in and sat down, with his eyes shining in their usual jovial way.

Knowing that Dr. Sabah had just traveled back home to Baghdad for the first time in years, I gushed, "How was it seeing home for the first time in so long?"

His smile faded, and pain etched his face instantly, changing his demeanor from bright to serious. He never held back the truth in joy or pain. "I was depressed, Diana. Seeing the destruction of my homeland and my neighborhood made me so deeply sad I didn't go out much." Militias had filled power vacuums left since the American withdrawal of troops, setting up impromptu sectarian checkpoints, which made travel a gamble he didn't know how to win.

After sharing the hard parts of going back, he dived into the things he loved: food I needed to try and the best restaurants to visit and the beauty of "Iraaaq" as he said with his signature lilting accent. Eyes twinkling, he raised his finger in the air and declared, "I am an Arab first and Muslim second." He explained that his "Arab molecule" was what gave him his enjoyment of people. The grand hospitality wasn't a chore; he delighted in eating, drinking, and sharing stories with people.

Hearing his infectious love for his people reminded me why Iraq had always been drawing me back: it was the people. Love for the people of Iraq was running in my veins now. I had been infected with the hospitality molecule that stretched my boundaries until no one was outside of them. People smiled and meant it. They whiled away hours with each other on purpose, because nothing was more important than offering each other presence and hospitality and tea—lots of tea. The Iraqis I met refused to see me as an enemy; my well-being was tied up in their well-being. So returning to Iraq wasn't optional for me.

Exhaling with relief, I left Dr. Sabah's office sure of two things. Like him, I would feel pain going back, but it would be laced with welcome. I loved my friends in Iraq. I wanted to be with them, even if I had to walk through my own battlefield to get there. I was going. And I'd have to be OK with bringing all of me—the baggage, the grief, and the unknown, along with a body that might see something, smell something, and shut down. Memories are flash floods. Some drown you and carry you away in a moment. Others, when they are done, leave you with a rainbow of unlikely hope. I was crossing my fingers for the rainbow.

I gathered up all the parts of me that would have to board the plane to Iraq. I wanted to wage peace in the place where I had waged war. I was a soldier who needed to return. I was a peacemaker who longed to meet the refugees and friends my Preemptive Love team had worked with for years. I longed to walk alongside them as they reclaimed their lives from war, violence, and ISIS. Iraq was the only other place I'd lived outside of Minnesota. I ached to see her in peacetime, to walk on a street without a Kevlar helmet and bulletproof vest. I wanted to see streets lined with cars and watermelon trucks instead of tanks. I wanted to see violence unmade and signs that life could be better. I was a mom who was raising my two sons to see themselves in another woman's son across the ocean.

I didn't know what I needed to carry home with me from the trip. But I was magnetically drawn toward going.

I also had the lure of spending time with my new friend. I had met her via email during the week I was hired at Preemptive Love. She reached out to me with a message introducing herself: "I'm Erin. I'm on the team in Iraq, and I'd love to get to know you." Since then, we hadn't stopped talking, via email, Skype, and our online meetings for work. She had worked as a photographer, museum curator, and antiques carpenter before joining Preemptive Love, and she was and is the fiercest peacemaker I knew. I loved her wild curly hair, raucous laughter, and practice of drawing in everyone around her. She carried scars from the violence of the world and chose to bear witness to unspeakable violence and the people it has wounded and left in its wake. I often felt safer surrounding myself with people who carry scars, because they are tender with mine. Even though Erin lived across the world, she had filled a place in my life. On the days when hearing about the violence experienced by our refugee friends in Iraq pushed me back into my own dark memories, she didn't flinch. She stepped right into the darkness with me. She even made herself a part of my kids' lives, sending them gifts at Christmas and surprising Bridger with a stack of his favorite books when he got Lyme disease and couldn't play outside during summer vacation.

To tell Erin of my decision to go, I called her via Skype. "You're coming!" she exclaimed. "Tell me what you want for breakfast, and you'll sleep in my bed, and I'll make up the couch for me." When I had gone to Iraq as a soldier, I didn't have a friend waiting to welcome me. For my second trip, Erin's presence in Iraq would change that. I had a welcome.

The night before I flew to Iraq, I stuffed cherry Pop-Tarts into the bulging pockets of my suitcase, smiling because Erin would go gaga over these treats. She and Bridger were the only people I knew whose eyes lit up like Christmas trees when pasty pink Pop-Tarts came out. Knowing someone wanted me to come to Iraq made this trip feel utterly different from the first time I had gone. That time, we landed in the middle of the night, with gas masks at the ready in case we were attacked. This time, I would be landing in Iraq in the middle of the night, but a friend would be waiting for me.

* * *

During my first days in Iraq, I drank endless cups of tea, curling up on plush cushions on the floor in a Syrian refugee camp, surrounded by stories and friends who were putting their lives back together after fleeing violence. The Preemptive Love Coalition was helping them create and launch businesses that gave them dignity instead of dependence. I knew these Iraqi and Syrian friends from staff calls, photos, and our videos. But this was the first time I met them in person.

Watching Nitchbeer smile and joke with her son as she buttoned his jeans, getting him ready for school, made me forget we were in a Syrian refugee camp. The early-morning sweetness between a mom and her son flooded the ten-foot-square cinder block room they lived in with warmth like sunshine. She had a fierce joy and a quick smile that drew me to her. It doesn't matter where you are, when you meet someone with that certain something, it's like you are already friends. I wished I spoke her language, so we could get on with the good conversations that you just can't have through an interpreter. She laughed as she recounted, "My son got up the other day, and when I told him there wasn't any school, he was mad at me because he loves school so much. I had to convince him it was Saturday, that I wasn't keeping him from school!"

160

After Nitchbeer got her son off to school and fed Erin and me treats she had brought from Syria, she led us to her mother-in-law's home. Walking down the dusty street reminded me of my friends in the village Awaijah—how a visit included the neighbor's house and then the next neighbor until I had drunk tea in every single home on the street. As we arrived at Nitchbeer's mother-in-law's house, shouts of "Erin!" circulated like popcorn as she was hugged and passed along to the next woman to greet. I remained standing at the door, as my shyness held me back from jumping into the introductions. I watched the conversation volley back and forth across the room. As we settled in and the tea was passed, conversation drifted to the same topics that women everywhere dive into when we get together without any men around: babies (having too many or struggling to have one), sex, and stories of our husbands. Peals of laughter filled the room, and women leaned onto each other's shoulders as they told the next story with bright eyes. Life is made up of the little things, and I was smack dab in the best life has to offer.

These women had fled ISIS in Syria. They had left the place that was home, carrying children and loss into Iraq. But even as they carried pain, they carried each other. They believed in each other. The mother-in-law was dubbed the Mayor. She knew which women in the camp needed health care or who needed a job, and she advocated for them until they got what they needed. As I turned to leave, she pushed into my hand a pair of slippers. Her skill at crocheting had launched a family business of making washcloths. Her eyebrows furrowed as she questioned the interpreter: "But do they fit her feet?" Even in gift giving, like a hawk, she made sure women got what they needed. The bright-green slippers fit me perfectly.

The next stop was the soap makers' house. A feast was laid out, and the faces were familiar. Preemptive Love had helped this family build and run their own business, making soap. They had become refugees after being targeted by ISIS for being Yezidi. This family survived, but they had lost babies, parents, and any sense of security while running for their lives to escape genocide.

I had been telling their story to divided faith communities across America. These congregations knew they had a call to care for the most vulnerable, like these refugees, but couldn't agree on how to do it. So I would show them pictures of Marwa making soap with her sister in the shipping container where they lived and then issue an invitation: "Buy their soap. Support these refugee friends as they remake their lives right where they are at." This was a relief for those who were fearful of refugees traveling to their country, settling in their neighborhoods, and sending children to school with their children. It stung to see a church refuse to love when love required them to share what they had, to see them wrestle with the command to love without having love for the other. But the opportunity to help by purchasing soap was great news for those who were desperate to respond to the needs they were seeing pile up in Iraq and Syria.

After telling the story of Marwa and her family for years, I felt like I knew them. Sitting shoulder to shoulder, I looked from face to face. This was my first time in their home, but it felt like home. I leaned back into the cushion and exhaled. Erin, who was talking with Marwa on my right, burst out laughing. The room was filled with my Preemptive Love teammates and their children, interspersed with three generations of Marwa's family. Hope was planted here. Family was so much bigger than I had realized.

After dinner, I followed a boy who was about my son's age up the stairs to the rooftop. He was one of Marwa's sons and had a mischievous twinkle in his eye. I thought the roof must be where the kids go to get away from the after-dinner chores. Dusk was turning the sky dark pink, bathing the dirt road in front of the house with golden light. Leaning against the railing, we smiled at each other as we spied a gaggle of girls chirping on the street below, passing a chip bag back and forth between them while they argued. Standing with Marwa's son in middle of his neighborhood, I was overcome with gratefulness that his life was just beginning. Violence didn't have the final say over his future; hope did.

* * *

A week later, as my time in Iraq was winding down, I received a message from my teammate Ihsan. "Diana, I would like for you to come to my house for dinner. I would be honored for you to meet my family." This was the invitation I had been hoping for since I first met Ihsan three years earlier. He was the only person on my team who lived in the province where I had been stationed during the war. I didn't want to leave Iraq without spending time with Ihsan and his family.

When the US Army had moved into his province, I was twenty-three years old and stationed a few villages away from his hometown, and Ihsan was seventeen years old. In another place or another time, we could have been on the same college campus. Instead, he and I had traveled the same roads, stopped at the same checkpoints, and driven through the same village squares. We shared an experience that few people do, although from the very different perspectives of an American soldier and an Iraqi civilian.

From communicating online, I knew that he had intelligent eyes, dark hair, and a smile so wide you almost fell into it. My colleagues told me that his wife was kind and movie-star gorgeous, that he doted on his four-year-old daughter, and that they had recently welcomed a new baby boy into the family.

As I walked up the stairwell to knock on his door, I nervously fingered the presents I brought for his daughter and son. His invitation into his home felt so big in a way I couldn't totally wrap my arms around. I wasn't sure what we would talk about or if I would have the courage to ask him about what wartime had been like for him. Or maybe we would drink tea and just play with his kids. My thoughts ran a mile a minute in the ten seconds it took between my knocking on the door and his answering.

As he opened the door, the smell of spicy sumac and warm bread filled the room. His wide smile made me forget my nerves. Standing beside him was his wife Zainab, a bright-pink scarf framing her petite head and shoulders. Taking my hand and pulling me into a shy hug, Zainab made me feel at home instantly. No one had exaggerated; she was movie-star gorgeous. "Muhammed!" I gushed as I put my arms out to hold their son. He wasn't a year old yet, but his arms and legs covered up half of his mom as she hoisted him up on her hip. Seeing him healthy was an answer to prayer. Months ago, a bad case of pneumonia had put him in the hospital, and Ihsan had asked for prayers for his baby boy to heal and come home from the hospital healthy. Seeing his bright eyes take in my curly hair and grab onto my earrings felt like a gift.

I felt a tug as four-year-old Rafeal, Ihsan and Zainab's daughter, pulled me into the living room, where she had been playing a game. I sat on the floor with her. Shyly, I pulled out the presents I had picked for her. They were all in English, and I worried she wouldn't like them. Her eyes lit up as she turned the pages of the book filled with princesses. The second present was a Candy Land game. Punching out the candy-colored playing cards, we set up the game. Before long, I stammered to Ihsan, "How is she beating me?" "She's only four, and the game is in English!"

He laughed and said, "YouTube, Diana. She's learned her colors in English by watching YouTube." His daughter's bright eyes danced as she moved her red Candy Land piece across the board and shouted, "Finished!" She had won.

Then we gathered around the table, and Zainab piled steaming dish after dish onto the table. The plates were filled and refilled as stories bounced back and forth. Watching Ihsan with his kids was magical. They captivated him; nothing made him light up more. They were his treasures. Rafeal could get him to swap food from his plate to hers with just one look and ended up sitting on his lap. As he beamed at her, I could see that there was nothing he loved more than indulging her. We commiserated about the lack of sleep during a baby's first year and discussed tricks to survive the evening fussy time.

Cozied around the table in his kitchen, I was still astonished at being there. Being welcomed into an Iraqi friend's home wasn't something I thought I would ever experience again after leaving the war. As I looked from face to face while holding baby Muhammed on my lap, this moment made me ache with joy. We had both been told to fear each other, to see each other as enemy. But here we were. I was holding his babies and sharing a meal in his home. And I knew he would be holding my babies if they were with me. This is what is possible when we refuse to see each other as enemy. Fifteen years after a bloody conflict, we have a relationship where we trust each other to hold our children.

After tea and dessert, the children meandered into the living room to play. With only adult ears around, I softly asked, "Ihsan, can I ask you something about the war?"

With the extravagant kindness that marked how he moved in the world, he reassured me, "Yes, Diana, anything." There were things

I remembered happening. Fifteen years later, I didn't know if what I remembered was true, a figment of my imagination, or too many experiences rolled up into one ball of memories. War is bewildering. I needed to poke my finger into it again and ask someone else who had been there, "Do you remember when US soldiers were torturing Iraqis in Abu Ghraib? What did you hear people saying? Toward the end of my deployment, my friends were telling me that soldiers from other countries, like the Italians, were abusing them. Was that true?"

We softly shared stories late into the night. Most everything I remembered, he said had really happened. Until Ihsan recounted the same stories, I didn't trust myself to fully wrap my hands around the memories as true. The landscape of the war had changed so quickly that month to month, the experience was completely different, almost unrelatable. His soft demeanor and humble nature gave me permission to ask him questions I wouldn't have asked anyone else.

With Ihsan, I wasn't alone anymore. We had both chosen a different way than most of our family, friends, and fellow countrymen were following. We both knew how it felt to have our loyalty questioned because of who we were willing to love. We both had been asked why we were helping "those people" or were friends with people others saw as the "other."

Ihsan fights for peace. He has decided to cross the lines drawn in the sand between Sunni and Shia, American and Iraqi, Christian and Muslim, those seen as worthy and those seen as disposable. He chooses everyone, no matter what line has been drawn around them. He has more courage, more compassion, and more hope for the future than anyone I know, even though he grew up seeing the violence done by those wearing the same uniform I did. He made a place for me at his family's table and invited me in.

Ihsan and I both knew war, but our children would know peace.

* * *

Coming home from Iraq the second time wasn't at all like the first. Making it through a war alive and coming back home felt like winning the lottery. At the same time, I felt terrified, knowing I was walking into a life I didn't recognize, because my eyes were different. No one who goes to war ever really comes back. I had lost things, had parts of myself taken away from me. Not all of me boarded the plane to come home. The war had also liberated me to love those I'd seen as an enemy. War gifted me with knowing what I would die for and what was worth living for: being the first to love every single time. And choosing to wage peace as if my life depended on it. But that new knowledge didn't match the worldviews of my friends, my family, or my faith community. And I knew it. The people waiting to welcome me home were expecting someone who didn't exist anymore. I didn't know how to navigate this minefield. I was excited to leave Iraq, but coming home a different person to a place that expected someone I wasn't felt so lonely it made me ache inside.

Stepping off the plane the second time felt like stepping into myself for the first time, as if I was meeting my whole self for the first time. Nothing was hidden, nothing tucked away. All of me was present and accounted for. Returning to Iraq was a time of wrapping my arms around the truest things I knew: I was a soldier and a peacemaker.

Now that I'm home, waging peace looks a lot different than it did on the battlefield of Iraq. But the question is still the same: What if you didn't have to choose between your country and the call to love? What if there was room at the table to be both a peacemaker and a patriot? How would we be different if we laid down our lives for our enemies as fiercely as we did for our friends?

I went to war knowing what I would die for. But now I know what I am living for: to be the first to love. Every single time.

Epilogue

This book has been seventeen years in the making, and I am honored you've taken the time to read my story. Maybe, as you read this story, you found yourself identifying with the commander who ordered me to run over an Iraqi child to protect soldiers in my unit—understanding that in a violent world, terrible choices are sometimes the only choices. Or maybe you heard yourself in the anger and judgment of the girl wearing the pink shirt at Samford University. I find myself in her words, too. I've thought ten times worse than she did when I was her age. I just wasn't as brave as she was to say it out loud.

Maybe you found yourself identifying with my extended family, who love their country so much they were blind to the humanity of the person at the receiving end of the bullets and bombs. They couldn't see another country's right to life or the human cost of their tradition of honorable service. I camped out there for most of my life.

Maybe you found yourself with your hand over your heart, pledging to the beautiful red, white, and blue flag in your worship space, but haven't noticed the white, dusty Christian flag standing in the corner, staking claim to a different kind of country, one where lions lie down with lambs and there is no violence, no flags, only one family.

Maybe you found yourself in the Iraqi grandmother, Om Hassan, who saw more to me than my uniform and battle rattle and who extended to me the bravest act of love I've ever received. She invited her enemy, armed and unknown, into the safety and security of her family's home. She chose me before I had the courage to choose her; she moved toward me before I would move toward her; she chose to trust me before she knew if I was trustworthy. She didn't see me as "other" so she could be disconnected from my humanity. She showed me what it looks like to belong to each other.

Maybe you found yourself in the soldier who assumed I was a conscientious objector because I was a medic and who decided his faith meant he couldn't take away another person's life or chance to know the Divine. His loyalty was to life, even if it cost him his death. Refusing to kill, he continued to show up and serve his country in one of the most dangerous jobs in the war, driving a truck full of supplies up and down the main supply routes.

Maybe you're wrestling with how you can love our country and serve in the armed forces while following God's call to love your enemy. Religious people have a long legacy of serving while respecting the sanctity of human life. Welcome, you are not alone. You won't find any statues built for soldiers who refuse to kill, but you will find yourself with something more valuable: peace.

Maybe you find yourself aching to return to a place or time, as I longed to return to Iraq—to revisit it and see it more alive, more whole and flourishing than it was when you left it. Maybe you want to wage peace where you waged war. You can. Maybe you can't go back to Iraq as I did. But you can go back to that friend you stopped talking to when they came out as queer. Maybe you can go back to the mother you avoided listening to as she told you how her children were hurt by racism in your school. Violence isn't only bombs and bullets; it can be speaking words that dehumanize and looking away when someone needs you to lean in and stand up alongside them to confront the racism, the intimidation, or the belittling. We can revisit those places by showing up to the person and saying, "I'm sorry. I should have done it differently back then. I want to listen and do better." Violence can be unmade when we are brave enough to choose a love that moves us toward those we've wronged instead of away.

Some of us have been immersed in a religious narrative that excludes LGBTQ people from access to God, or rightness, or protection from violence and discrimination. I was immersed in that narrative, too. It's time to reexamine and hold to the light the things we've been handed down. Sometimes even those we love are handing us dirty water, believing that it is sparkling clear, unaware of the harm they are causing. It's our responsibility to sift the beliefs we've been given through the lens of self-sacrificing love—because it's not love if it only serves itself.

Maybe you've been handed the narrative of nationalism, which puts value on only the lives and children born inside your border. Waging peace means we erase lines that tell us whose children are worthy to survive and whose children are disposable. Maybe you feel a particular joy or security at having been born in the "right" country, in the "right" religion, or on the "right" side of history. I was there, too. I sang "Proud to Be an American" on the Fourth of July, pounding my feet into the Iraqi sand, bursting with pride. I felt like I loved America more than anybody else that day, because I had boots on the ground and a weapon strapped to my hip. But instead of serving those who gathered under the American flag, my pride used my service to co-opt the flag, to make it more mine than yours. I believed my religion held more weight and my politics were more valid than yours. Veterans should never use their service to make themselves greater than the people they serve. I'm embarrassed that I found myself there for a while.

I find parts of myself standing in each of these places and perspectives. It took a war to shatter the singular lens of "us versus them." It took meeting the people I had been told were my enemy in war in order to value those I'd been told were my enemy back home where I lived. Before the war, I viewed the world through lenses obscured by false patriotism, white supremacy, and self-centered religion. I didn't even know I was wearing these glasses or seeing the world through them until I went to war and saw my beliefs in action. Bullets and bombs cleared my ears to the still, soft voice of the Divine: "But I love them, Diana. I love them, too." It took being faced with the choice of whether to take a child's life to make me able to surrender to the undeniable call to love my enemies. That was the first time I felt pulled between what God was asking of me and what my country required of me. God wasn't calling out my bad theology; God was confronting my unlove.

But I never imagined that the real test would come when I returned home. How would love respond to the divides in my neighborhood or the violence that took the lives of Tamir Rice, Trayvon Martin, Michael Brown, and so many others? What could love say to the fear and demonizing that infected every news headline, painting the sky with "us versus them" ultimatums? Could love stand up to the vandalism and bombings of black churches, mosques, and Jewish cemeteries? What could love say to the white-supremacist rally in Charlottesville and the white-nationalist recruiting in my city? Could preemptive love respond to the voices of my scared and marginalized black, brown, indigenous, and Muslim neighbors? Could it answer my own son's question, "Did you know you were bringing me into a racist country when you adopted me?"

If choosing to love first can change enemies into friends on the battlefield of Iraq, I know that it can right here, in our neighborhoods, churches, and families, who are battling over politics, religion, migrants at the border, and who belongs in America. Love is the foundation I'm planting my feet squarely on.

I had no control over what the Iraq War would ask of me; the only thing I could decide was how I would show up in it. What I would do. What I wouldn't do. In that decision, I found what was worth dying for and what was worth living for: love.

Love is what I am arming my sons with to go out in an angry and hurting world. This is the truest gift I can give them—an arrow to load in their bow and a solid bull's-eye to aim at. It's a posture to live from, to love from. It's the power to decide ahead of time how they will show up for the neighbor nobody likes and how they will respond to the bully on the playground or to the violence and uncertainty this world is going to ambush them with.

I can't guarantee that choosing to love their friends *and* their enemies isn't going to cost them. I can't tell them they are going to win, get ahead, or avoid pain. But I can tell them there is no greater freedom than refusing to harm another person. And that's a freedom worth fighting for.

Freedom isn't free, no matter what country we are born into. The amount of violence against other human beings we are willing to accept is a litmus test for our own freedom. We can measure our unlove by the distance we put between ourselves and the violence done to others. The currency of unlove is dealt in indifference. Free people are able give their lives away, give the advantage away, or put another's safety or concern above their own. That's true freedom.

Fear tells us to insulate ourselves from others. Ignorance convinces us to ignore others and their problems. Self-righteousness tempts us to create us-versus-them lines, keeping all the truth and goodness on our side. Self-righteousness separates because if we were connected, we might have to share our righteousness or worthiness with others. Turning a blind eye to another group's oppression or experience of violence is self-protection. Refusing to acknowledge the historical trauma of those around us is a cultural tradition many of us have been handed down, generation to generation, forming our foundation of erasing wrongs so we don't have to *right* them. But we can change these traditions and narratives.

The world can change, because we can change. I have so much hope for you. I have so much hope for me.

I am fighting for your freedom and my freedom. We must have brave conversations. We must find out what we don't know. Waging peace requires that we have the courage to face what's broken—first in ourselves and then in the systems affecting those around us—and uncover who has been harmed and how we are connected to them. Because we are intertwined together. Love speaks the truth of the harm done, while unshakable goodness holds space for the offender at the table. We all have a seat at the peacemaking table. Love is refusing to take away an oppressor's chair at the family table while taking the stick of violence out of their hand, because violence ricochets and is absorbed by the most vulnerable and marginalized among us. It's time to center their pain and to put ourselves between them and the violence.

I don't know what your journey of peacemaking will look like. But for me, I'm never going to stop learning and restoring, as well as listening to and standing with those in pain. I am part of why another person is in pain, which means I can also be part of another person's peace. I am complicit in parts of my own pain, which means I can be part of rebuilding my own peace.

That is my wild hope that catches my eye and makes my heart beat fast.

I'll never stop acknowledging the pain of others, because empathy is the flashlight leading us toward wholeness and healing. If we ignore those in our world and neighborhoods who are in pain, we will ignore our own healing and suffocate our own hope, because we are connected to each other.

Waging peace is believing that the best for another person is the best for myself, my country, and my world.

You can build something new, one person, one relationship, one meal at a time. You can build friendships instead of watering the flowers next to our long-held fences.

You can choose to believe in the unshakable goodness of those across the pew or political divide.

You can choose fierce kindness by speaking the truth to people about the impact their decisions make on the vulnerable.

You can call self-supremacy the liar it is. It's a bait and switch. Putting ourselves first, our kids first, our faith first, our country first only creates us-versus-them dividing lines. It may even draw battle lines. Its sells us the snake oil of scarcity. It will never give us the country, the neighborhood, or the world we want for our children. Only love can do that.

Run toward love as if your life depends on it. Because it does.